Beginning CSS Preprocessors

With Sass, Compass, and Less

Anirudh Prabhu

Apress®

Beginning CSS Preprocessors: With SASS, Compass.js, and Less.js

ISBN-13 (pbk): 978-1-4842-1348-3

ISBN-13 (electronic): 978-1-4842-1347-6

Trademarked names, logos, and images may appear in this book. Rather than use a trademark symbol with every occurrence of a trademarked name, logo, or image we use the names, logos, and images only in an editorial fashion and to the benefit of the trademark owner, with no intention of infringement of the trademark.

The use in this publication of trade names, trademarks, service marks, and similar terms, even if they are not identified as such, is not to be taken as an expression of opinion as to whether or not they are subject to proprietary rights.

While the advice and information in this book are believed to be true and accurate at the date of publication, neither the authors nor the editors nor the publisher can accept any legal responsibility for any errors or omissions that may be made. The publisher makes no warranty, express or implied, with respect to the material contained herein.

Managing Director: Welmoed Spahr
Acquisitions Editor: Celestin Suresh John
Development Editor: Matthew Moodie
Technical Reviewer: Lokesh Iyer
Editorial Board: Steve Anglin, Pramilla Balan, Louise Corrigan, James DeWolf, Jonathan Gennick, Robert Hutchinson, Celestin Suresh John, Michelle Lowman, James Markham, Susan McDermott, Matthew Moodie, Jeffrey Pepper, Douglas Pundick, Ben Renow-Clarke, Gwenan Spearing
Coordinating Editor: Rita Fernando
Copy Editor: Kezia Endsley
Compositor: SPi Global
Indexer: SPi Global

Distributed to the book trade worldwide by Springer Science+Business Media New York, 233 Spring Street, 6th Floor, New York, NY 10013. Phone 1-800-SPRINGER, fax (201) 348-4505, e-mail orders-ny@springer-sbm.com, or visit www.springer.com. Apress Media, LLC is a California LLC and the sole member (owner) is Springer Science + Business Media Finance Inc (SSBM Finance Inc). SSBM Finance Inc is a Delaware corporation.

For information on translations, please e-mail rights@apress.com, or visit www.apress.com.

Apress and friends of ED books may be purchased in bulk for academic, corporate, or promotional use. eBook versions and licenses are also available for most titles. For more information, reference our Special Bulk Sales–eBook Licensing web page at www.apress.com/bulk-sales.

Any source code or other supplementary material referenced by the author in this text is available to readers at www.apress.com/. For detailed information about how to locate your book's source code, go to www.apress.com/source-code/.

Contents at a Glance

Contents

About the Author

Anirudh Prabhu is a software engineer with over six years of industry experience. He specializes in technologies such as HTML5, CSS3, PHP, jQuery, Twitter Bootstrap, Less, and Sass, and he also has knowledge of CoffeeScript and AngularJS. In addition to web development, he has been involved in building training materials and writing tutorials for these technologies.

About the Technical Reviewer

Lokesh Iyer completed his bachelor's in IT from KC College, Mumbai and received his MBA from Sydenham College, Mumbai. He is the founder and director of SI Technologies, a company focused on providing hardware and software solutions as well as web exposure and security solutions. Over the past three years, he completed over 60 projects on HTML5, CSS3, JavaScript, jQuery, PHP, C#, Android, and MySQL/SQLite databases with his team. Apart from his business ventures, he is a visiting faculty member at KC College of the bachelor's in IT program.

Acknowledgments

First and foremost, I wish thank the awesome team at Apress for offering me such a wonderful opportunity to write this book. When Celestin "discovered" me through LinkedIn and asked me if I would like to write a book, it sounded like a straight and easy task. Over the next month, he painstakingly guided me through the entire process of preparing an initial proposal for the book and helped me finalize it. Subsequently, when the real action started in terms of writing the chapters, Rita was always there. She was the scrum master who was always there to help. She gave me that gentle nudge to make sure that even as I was running behind schedule, I did everything that needed to be done to catch up and deliver the chapter in potentially shippable increments. Thanks, Celestin and Rita, for not giving up on me!

I also want to thanks Matt Moodie and the large team from Apress working in background, for all their efforts. In addition, the review feedback and critical inputs by reviewers is an author's lifeline—it is the first feedback on a product that is still quite raw. I want to offer my sincere thanks to Lokesh Iyer for his technical review.

I can't thank my professional network enough for enriching my learning journey through the years—my former employers, my clients, managers, colleagues, team members, students, readers of my blog, audience to my talks, and the noblest of them all— the fellow volunteers. Thanks for all the support and learning opportunities and for making me a better professional every single day.

Finally, despite all the diligent efforts of the editorial team and reviewers, I must accept responsibility for all the mistakes and shortcomings in this book. Let me know how I can make this book better.

Introduction

CSS preprocessor came into buzz a couple of years ago. The concept intrigued me: Allowing use of preprocessor files that could contain one or several things like variables, functions, mixins, and the like. After development, these special files would then be compiled into regular CSS files that all web browsers could understand.

Being a believer of phrase "if it's not broken, don't fix it," I avoided using CSS preprocessors. The initial thought that would come to my mind was, "Why add unnecessary processes to my workflow?". Also, I feared the steep learning curve and the command-line interface provided me another reason to avoid CSS preprocessors.

Finally, after watching several podcasts and reading through many articles, I had an "a-ha" moment. It made me realize that, "Wow, I should be incorporating this in my workflow!".

Since then, I've been using Sass and Less in my projects, and it seems to have made my development a lot simpler and more efficient. In this book, you will learn how both of these preprocessors work.

You'll first start by learning about the concept of preprocessors and how they work. You also learn about the popular flavors of preprocessors available on the market. You then look into the GUI-based tools available for people who are not familiar with command-line interfaces.

As the chapters progress, you will learn all about these two preprocessors—Sass and Less—and learn about a popular framework based on Sass called Compass.

The knowledge shared in this book can help you improve your productivity and write maintainable and scalable CSS code.

■ ■ ■

## CHAPTER 1

Introduction to Preprocessors

HTML5 and CSS3 are changing how web pages are designed. CSS3 provided web developers with advanced features such as gradients, transitions, and animations, etc. However, these new features increased the complexity of CSS code, thus making it more difficult to maintain.

Besides the complexity introduced by CSS3, writing CSS may turn painful with time, because programmers have to perform many of the same activities over and over again (such as having to look up color values in CSS and margin/padding declarations). These small repetitive tasks add up to quite a bit of inefficiency. Preprocessors are the solution to these, and a handful of other, inefficiencies.

CSS preprocessors extend CSS with modern programming-language concepts. In order to use Sass (Syntactically Awesome Stylesheets), you must know how to code in CSS. CSS preprocessors allow you to use variables, functions, operations, and even rule or selector nesting while coding your CSS. With CSS preprocessors, you can apply the "Don't Repeat Yourself" (DRY) principle to your CSS code. Following the DRY principle helps you avoid code repetition.

What Are Preprocessors?

A preprocessor takes one form of data and converts it to another. In the context of CSS, Less and Sass are popular preprocessor languages, and they take input in the Less or SCSS format and produce processed CSS.

These CSS preprocessors empower CSS by removing the inefficiencies and making web sites easier and more logical to build. The increase in popularity of preprocessors led to the rise of different frameworks based on them; one of the more popular is Compass.

Figure 1-1 shows how a preprocessor takes a preprocessor-formatted file and translates it to CSS that the browser understands.

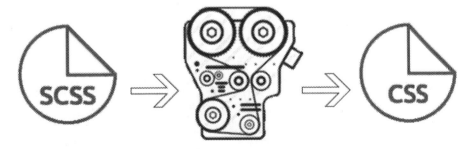

Figure 1-1. *Preprocessor-friendly file being translated to normal CSS*

With a preprocessor, you can structure CSS similar to other languages like PHP or JavaScript. Thus, a preprocessor brings peace of mind to the developer. It lets you write code that's future-proof and easily maintainable, thus saving time and energy.

Preprocessors are extensions of CSS, which means that valid CSS code is valid preprocessor code. Developers familiar with CSS won't have a learning curve while learning any preprocessor.

Why Use Preprocessors?

CSS uses a declarative form of programming. This means that the styles that you write in the code are used directly by the browser, without any compiling.

Many developers prefer to write stylesheets by hand. They believe that preprocessors would add extra complexity to their workflow or would have a steep learning curve. But in reality, CSS preprocessors make your daily work a lot easier. This book shows you how preprocessors can be more efficient for writing CSS without disturbing your workflow.

Let's consider an example where you need to replace multiple instances of a color that's used sitewide by finding it one instance at a time. Wouldn't it be great if CSS could simplify this process? Something like Listing 1-1 would be an example.

Listing 1-1. Reusable Variable for Color

```
$site-color:#eee;

a {
        color: $site-color;
}
#topBar {
        background-color: $site-color;
        color:#fff;
}
```

With a preprocessor, changing a value in one place changes the entire stylesheet. This is shown in Listing 1-2.

Listing 1-2. Output of Listing 1-1

```
a {
  color: #eee;
}

#topBar {
  background-color: #eee;
  color: #fff;
}
```

Let's consider another example of code repetition. Many times there are blocks of code used at various locations in your stylesheet, as shown in Listing 1-3.

Listing 1-3. Repeated Code Block

```
p{
        padding-bottom:45px;
        text-align:center;
}
footer {
        padding-bottom:45px;
        text-align:center;
}
```

With preprocessors, you can put these redundant rules into a *mixin*, which is defined once and can be included as needed. This is shown in Listing 1-4.

Listing 1-4. Creating and Using a Reusable Code Block in the Preprocessor

```
@mixin containerSettings {
        padding-bottom: 45px;
        text-align:center;
}
p {
        @include containerSettings;
}
footer {
        @include containerSettings;
}
```

Listing 1-5. Output of Listing 1-4

```
p {
  padding-bottom: 45px;
  text-align: center;
}

footer {
  padding-bottom: 45px;
  text-align: center;
}
```

CSS, which is the foundation of all preprocessors, has a steep learning curve when it comes to understanding how different properties work, understanding cascading, browser support for various properties, the selectors, the quirks, and so forth. In addition to all the previous points, consider that maintaining stylesheets in today's complex interfaces is a big challenge too.

Most of the time, stylesheets are immensely repetitive, with properties or groupings of properties, etc. The typical CSS file is a linear document. This makes a programmer from an object-oriented domain go crazy.

As per the DRY principle: *Every piece of knowledge must have a single, unambiguous, authoritative representation in a system.*

The simplest explanation of this is that redundancy in code can result in failure and can create confusion for developers. CSS does not follow the DRY principle. Most of the times, CSS files will contain repeated rules, declarations, and values. Developers are constantly writing the same snippets of code throughout their stylesheets.

CSS lacks features like variables, symbolic constants, conditionals, expressions over variables, and so on, that are available in all other programming languages.

The CSS preprocessor sits between your preprocessor-friendly file and the compiled CSS files, which will be served to the browser. CSS preprocessors allow you to write code as per the DRY principle, making it faster, efficient, and maintainable. The code is then compiled into regular CSS files via the command line or an application.

Consider the example in Listing 1-6. Modern browsers support RGBA (Red Green Blue Alpha) and HSLA (Hue Saturation Lightness Alpha) color values. However, you need to provide a fallback for older browsers. A common practice is to declare a hex value first and then the RGBA or HSLA value.

Listing 1-6. Supporting a New Color Format in All Browsers Using CSS

```
.container {
  background-color: #000;
  background-color: rgba(0,0,0, 0.9);
}
```

With preprocessors, this job can be done easily. If the same task were to be completed using the Sass precompiler, it would be done as shown in Listing 1-7.

Listing 1-7. Sass Version of Listing 1-6

```
$black:#000;
.container {
        background-color: $black;
        background-color: rgba($black, 0.9);
}
```

The preprocessor does all the calculations related to RGBA values for you.

With arrival of CSS3 support in modern browsers, people are not using images as much and are going with pure CSS. However, each browser has its own implementation of these features, and therefore these require vendor prefixes and different syntaxes. You can see a simple example of this in Listing 1-8.

Listing 1-8. Implementation of CSS Features for Different Browsers

```
.container {
        -webkit-border-radius: 10px;
        -moz-border-radius: 10px;
        -ms-border-radius: 10px;
        -o-border-radius: 10px;
        border-radius: 10px;
}
```

Preprocessors make this job easier by allowing you to declare this code in a reusable component called a *mixin* (covered in coming chapters) and then use it directly in your code.

This example assumes that this reusable mixin is named `rounded-corners`. The code for this in the Sass preprocessor would look like Listing 1-9.

Listing 1-9. Implementing the code of Listing 1-8 Using a Sass Preprocessor

```
.container {
  @include rounded-corners(4px);
}
```

So far you have seen how preprocessors help in coding CSS. Now let's consider how preprocessors can help during the post-coding phase. Compressing the CSS reduces its original size, which results in less loading time. This can be done using online tools or editor addons.

However, the preprocessor can compile to CSS in various ways, one of which is compressed. The preprocessor can be configured in a way that, whenever a preprocessor file is saved, it is automatically compiled into CSS and compressed. This makes it production ready.

Misconceptions About CSS Preprocessors

This section discusses some common misconceptions that prevent developers from adopting preprocessors in their daily workflow.

You Need To Be a Command-Line Expert

Many developers fear the command line. To use preprocessors, you require very little command-line knowledge. In fact, you need to learn only a single command. Additionally, there are applications that perform the same task without accessing the command line.

You Need To Change the Way You Write CSS

Developers have a way of writing stylesheets and organizing them. Since the SCSS syntax is the same as CSS, developers don't need to change the way they have been writing CSS.

Why Not Write CSS Directly?

The initial reaction of many developers when looking at CSS preprocessors is, "What's wrong with writing the CSS directly? We use CSS regularly and can fix all the usual layout issues and develop responsive web sites that work across all devices."

Well, preprocessors by themselves cannot produce better CSS. For example, if you lack knowledge as to how to use CSS, preprocessors won't be of any use in solving your issues. Preprocessors help you write CSS in a fast and maintainable manner by adhering to the DRY principle.

Which Are the Known Preprocessors?

Let's look at some known preprocessors available today, shown in Figure 1-2.

Figure 1-2. *Known preprocessing frameworks*

Sass

Sass (Syntactically Awesome Stylesheets) is the most famous preprocessor and it's been around for eight years. Sass is a preprocessor language originally designed and developed by Hampton Catlin and Natalie Weizenbaum.

When SassScript is compiled, it generates CSS rules for various selectors as specified in the Sass file. Sass can monitor the .sass or .scss files and generate an output .css file whenever the .sass or .scss file is saved.

Sass is open source and coded in Ruby.

Less

Just like Sass, Less is another popular CSS preprocessor. It enhances the default CSS syntax by provision of mixins, variables, and nested style rules. It is easy to set up. You can also reference its JavaScript file in your HTML document and get started.

Less has attracted a very strong userbase due to its simplicity. Less is open source. Its initial version was written in Ruby; however, the later versions were written in JavaScript. A valid CSS code is a valid Less code, because Less follows the same semantics.

The main difference between Less and other CSS preprocessors is that Less allows real-time compilation via `less.js` within the browser.

Compass

Compass is an open source CSS authoring framework. Compass is based on Sass, and hence it can use of all Sass' features. It is very popular and is under active development. With Compass, developers can write cleaner markup without presentational classes.

Compass is filled with many reusable patterns most commonly used by developers.

In parallel to Compass is Bourbon, which is built with Sass, for Sass by Thoughtbot. Bourbon is a library of simple and lightweight mixins for Sass.

Some of key features that Compass provides are discussed next.

Mixins

Compass and Bourbon both provide a huge collection of mixins for various CSS3 features, which you will look at in detail in coming chapters. That means the developers don't have to worry about vendor prefixes or CSS hacks. Listing 1-10 demonstrates the use of mixins with regard to box sizing.

Listing 1-10. Example Showing the Use of a Mixin Provided by Compass

```
el{
        @include box-sizing(border-box);
}
```

Typography

Compass and Bourbon both contain typography-related mixins, variables, and functions. Compass comes with a lot of variables and a couple of mixins.

One of the features of Compass in this area is that it can also work with rem units with px fallbacks.

Listing 1-11. Example Showing Use Typographical Functionalities of Compass

```
el{
        @include adjust-font-size-to(42px);
}
```

Helpers

One thing that Compass provides are helpers. Helpers save time, as they are predefined CSS snippets that you need to use directly in your stylesheets.

For example, Compass provides a helper for clearing the floats, a reset (with various options), some techniques for image replacement, and more.

Bourbon calls these helpers addons, and they are fewer in number than Compass.

Sprites

Because Compass is partly built in Ruby, Compass can interact with the file system. One of the things it can do is build sprites based on a folder of images.

Listing 1-12. Example Showing Compass' Simple Way of Building Sprites

```
@import "icon/*.png";
@include all-icon-sprites;
```

It also provides functions like image-width(), image-height(), and inline-image(), which encode an image file in Base64.

Features of Preprocessors

This section goes through some common features of preprocessors that make them great tools for developers versus using CSS directly. You will be looking at some examples in context. The examples use two famous preprocessors—Sass and Less—which you will be studying in detail in coming chapters.

Variables

Variables help you store information that needs to be reused in your stylesheet. Properties like colors, font styles, or any CSS style can be stored and reused. For example, in Sass $ symbol is used to declare a variable.

Listing 1-13. Example Showing Implementation of Variables Using SASS

```
$text-color:#333;
body {
        color:$text-color;
}
```

When this code is compiled, it takes the variable defined for the $text-color and outputs normal CSS with the variable's values placed in the CSS. This can be useful when working with properties applicable sitewide and keeping them consistent throughout the site.

Listing 1-14. Output of Previous Code Snippet

```
body {
        color:#333;
}
```

Similarly in Less CSS @ symbol is used to declare a variable.

Listing 1-15. Example Showing Implementation of Variables Using Less

```
@text-color:#333;
body{
        color:$text-color;
}
```

Nesting

Visual hierarchy of a page is not as clear in CSS as it is in HTML. Preprocessors let you nest CSS selectors, similar to the way it is done in HTML.

Listing 1-16. Example of Nesting in Sass or Less

```
nav {
  ul {
    margin: 0 auto;
    padding: 10px 15px;
    list-height: 1em;
  }
}
```

The generated CSS will look like Listing 1-17.

Listing 1-17. Output of Previous Code Snippet

```
nav ul {
  margin: 0 auto;
  padding: 10px 15px;
  list-height: 1em;
}
```

Import

Preprocessors have a slightly different @import implementation to the one in CSS. Instead of fetching a file from server, Sass will fetch the specified file and merge it into the file you're importing. This results in a single CSS file being served to the web browser.

Suppose you have two SCSS files called reset.scss and style.scss and you want to import reset.scss into style.scss. This can be done using Sass; see Listing 1-18.

Listing 1-18. Example of Importing Content of One File into Another

```
@import 'reset';
body {
        background-color: #cfcfcf;
}
```

▓ **Note** There is no need to specify the file extension while importing files in Sass. Sass automatically figures out the appropriate file and imports it.

In Less, however, the behavior of import varies per file extension. If the imported file has a .css extension, it will be treated as a normal CSS import and won't be changed when compiled. If it has any other extension, it will be treated like Less and will be imported and merged.

Mixins

Mixins let you create snippets of CSS declarations that you can reuse throughout your stylesheet. Mixins are further configurable by passing parameters as well as setting defaults for those parameters. Mixins are most useful when you want to repeatedly use vendor-prefixed syntax. They reduce the tedious rewriting of code (see Listings 1-19 and 1-20).

Listing 1-19. Example of a Border-Radius Mixin with a Parameter and its Default Value in Sass

```
@mixin rounded-corners($radius:5px) {
  -webkit-border-radius: $radius;
    -moz-border-radius: $radius;
     -ms-border-radius: $radius;
         border-radius: $radius;
}

.container { @include rounded-corners(10px); }
```

Listing 1-20. Example of a Border-Radius Mixin with a Parameter and its Default Value in Less

```
.rounded-corners(@radius:5px) {
  -webkit-border-radius: @radius;
    -moz-border-radius: @radius;
     -ms-border-radius: @radius;
         border-radius: @radius;
}

.container { .rounded-corners(10px); }
```

Extend/Inheritance

Preprocessors allow you to share a collection of CSS properties between one or more selectors. This helps you write preprocessor code as per the DRY principle. See Listings 1-21 and 1-22.

Listing 1-21. Example for Extend in Sass

```
.messagebox {
        font-size:1em;
        line-height:40px;
}

.successBox {
        @extend .messagebox;
        color:#0F0;
}
```

Listing 1-22. Example for Extend in Less

```
.messagebox {
        font-size:1em;
        line-height:40px;
}

.successBox {
        &:extend(.messagebox);
        color:#0F0;
}
```

Operators

Preprocessors provide standard math operators so that you can perform calculations on the fly. See Listing 1-23.

Listing 1-23. Example Showing a Math Operation in Sass and Less

```
.mainContent {
  float: left;
  width: 750px / 960px * 100%;
}
```

Problems with CSS Preprocessors

This section discusses the features of preprocessors that are used inappropriately. You will see most common problems that occur due to misuse or overuse of preprocessor features.

Problems with Mixins

Mixins are reusable blocks of code that are called wherever you need to include them. This is instead of having to rewrite these blocks several times.

Consider a code snippet written in the Sass preprocessor, shown in Listing 1-24.

Listing 1-24. An Example of a Mixin Using Sass

```
@mixin notification {
    color: #fff;
    border-radius: 50%;
}

.errorNotification {
    @include notification;
    background:#F00;
}

.successNotification {
    @include notification;
    background: #0F0;
}
```

This code compiles to Listing 1-25.

Listing 1-25. Output of Listing 1-24

```
.errorNotification {
  color: #fff;
  border-radius: 50%;
  background: #F00;
}

.successNotification {
  color: #fff;
  border-radius: 50%;
  background: #0F0;
}
```

Notice the code duplication that occurs in the output shown in Listing 1-25. If this mixin is used extensively across style code, it would result in a large amount of code redundancy and thus increase the file size.

Sass has an alternative approach, which is not supported by other preprocessors—*extending*. Extending the code will set the same properties of multiple selectors simultaneously, by specifying the selectors in a comma-separated format.

This approach avoids duplication; however, it can cause performance issues if too many selectors are extended. The resulting CSS will have many selectors in comma-separated format, which can cause performance issues.

Extending Selectors or Using Mixins Can Hamper Maintenance

Extending classes or using mixins can cause maintenance issues. Since the properties are declared and used in different places, the chances of changing a property without anticipating a complete impact are high. This can cause layouts to break at any point.

Summary

This chapter introduced preprocessors. You looked at how they can influence your workflow, making it more efficient and far easier to maintain in the future. You also looked at some known preprocessors currently available in the market.

The next chapter dives into Sass and discusses its various features.

CHAPTER 2

■ ■ ■

Introduction to Sass

In the previous chapter, you learned about precompilers, including why to use them, which ones are the known preprocessors, and their features. This chapter covers one of the most popular preprocessors: Sass.

In this chapter, you explore the following aspects of Sass:

- Installation
- Running the code
- Variables
- Comments
- Data types
- Parentheses
- Nested rules
- Nested properties
- Referencing parent selector
- Interpolation
- Placeholder selector
- Logical and control directives

Installing Sass

You install Sass via a Ruby gem, so you need to have Ruby installed on your machine. If you are on Mac OS X, you already have Ruby installed. If you are on Windows or Linux, you need to download and install Ruby from http://rubyinstaller.org/downloads/.

After installing Ruby, you install Sass by running the gem command. gem can be thought of as an extension that extends the functionality of applications that consume Ruby. You can install Sass via the command line using the command shown in Listing 2-1. A simple interpretation of this command is "Ruby, install the gem called sass".

Listing 2-1. Command for Installing Sass

```
sudo gem install sass
```

After installation completes, you can verify it by running the command in Listing 2-2.

Listing 2-2. Command for Verifying Sass Installation

```
sass -v
```

This should give you the output shown in Figure 2-1.

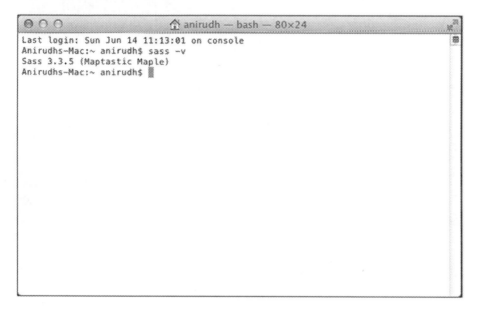

Figure 2-1. *Output of the sass-v command*

Upon completing this installation, you are ready to use Sass.

Checking Other Versions of Sass

You can check for other available versions, beside latest version, by executing the command shown in Listing 2-3.

Listing 2-3. Checking for Other Versions of Sass

```
gem list sass -a -r
```

This command asks Ruby to list all the gems that have "sass" in their name. The -r command attribute tells Ruby to check it remotely, where all Sass versions are available. The -a command attribute is for listing all available versions.

The output of this gem list command is shown in Listing 2-4.

Listing 2-4. Output Text of gem list Command

```
sass (3.4.18, 3.4.17, 3.4.16, 3.4.15, 3.4.14, 3.4.13, 3.4.12, 3.4.11, 3.4.10, 3.4.9, 3.4.8,
3.4.7, 3.4.6, 3.4.5, 3.4.4, 3.4.3, 3.4.2, 3.4.1, 3.4.0, 3.3.14, 3.3.13, 3.3.12, 3.3.11,
3.3.10, 3.3.9, 3.3.8, 3.3.7, 3.3.6, 3.3.5, 3.3.4, 3.3.3, 3.3.2, 3.3.1, 3.3.0, 3.2.19,
3.2.18, 3.2.17, 3.2.16, 3.2.15, 3.2.14, 3.2.13, 3.2.12, 3.2.11, 3.2.10, 3.2.9, 3.2.8, 3.2.7,
3.2.6, 3.2.5, 3.2.4, 3.2.3, 3.2.2, 3.2.1, 3.2.0, 3.1.21, 3.1.20, 3.1.19, 3.1.18, 3.1.17,
3.1.16, 3.1.15, 3.1.14, 3.1.13, 3.1.12, 3.1.11, 3.1.10, 3.1.9, 3.1.8, 3.1.7, 3.1.6, 3.1.5,
3.1.4, 3.1.3, 3.1.2, 3.1.1, 3.1.0)
sass-960gs (1.0.0, 0.1.0, 0.0.3, 0.0.2, 0.0.1)
sass-a11y (0.1.0)
sass-aleksi (0.1.2)
sass-align (0.1.1, 0.1.0)
sass-buttons (0.1.2, 0.1.1)
sass-capucine (0.0.3, 0.0.2, 0.0.1)
sass-color-helpers (2.0.0)
sass-color-schemes (0.4.0, 0.3.1, 0.3.0, 0.2.0, 0.1.0)
sass-extractor (0.0.1)
sass-extras (1.1.0, 1.0.2, 1.0.1, 1.0.0, 0.0.1)
sass-flexi (1.0.6, 1.0.5, 1.0.4, 1.0.3, 1.0.2, 1.0.1, 1.0.0)
sass-fontimage (0.1.1, 0.1.0)
sass-getunicode (1.0, 0.0.2, 0.0.1, 0.0.0)
sass-globbing (1.1.1, 1.1.0, 1.0.0)
sass-globbing-pr-20 (1.1.2)
sass-images (0.0.2, 0.0.1)
sass-import_once (0.1.3, 0.1.2, 0.1.0)
sass-json-vars (0.3.3, 0.3.2, 0.3.1, 0.3.0, 0.2.1, 0.2.0, 0.1.0, 0.0.1)
sass-list-maps (1.0.0, 0.9.9, 0.9.7, 0.9.6, 0.9.5, 0.9.3, 0.9.2, 0.9.1)
sass-material-colors (0.0.5, 0.0.4.2, 0.0.4.1, 0.0.4, 0.0.3, 0.0.2, 0.0.1)
sass-media_query_combiner (0.0.7, 0.0.6, 0.0.5, 0.0.4, 0.0.3, 0.0.2, 0.0.1)
sass-mediaqueries-rails (1.3, 1.2.3.1, 1.2.3)
sass-mixin-collection-rails (0.0.11, 0.0.1)
sass-pantones (0.0.1)
sass-pygments-rails (0.1)
sass-rails (5.0.4, 5.0.3, 5.0.2, 5.0.1, 5.0.0, 4.0.5, 4.0.4, 4.0.3, 4.0.2, 4.0.1, 4.0.0,
3.2.6, 3.2.5, 3.2.4, 3.2.3, 3.2.2, 3.2.1, 3.2.0, 3.1.7, 3.1.6, 3.1.5, 3.1.4, 3.1.3, 3.1.2,
3.1.1, 3.1.0)
sass-rails-bootstrap (2.2.2.3, 2.2.2.2, 2.2.2.1, 2.2.2, 2.2.1, 2.1.1, 2.1.0.1, 2.1.0, 2.0.4,
2.0.2)
sass-rails-source-maps (0.1.0, 0.0.4, 0.0.3, 0.0.2, 0.0.1)
sass-rails3 (4.0.1)
```

You can also determine which prerelease versions are available by executing the command shown in Listing 2-5.

Listing 2-5. Checking the Prerelease Version Through the Command Line

```
gem list sass -pre -r
```

You can install the prerelease version if you want to try out all the bleeding-edge features that are not available in stable releases. Use the command shown in Listing 2-6 to do so.

Listing 2-6. Installing the Prerelease Version

```
sudo gem install sass -pre
```

There may be situations where you might need to uninstall existing versions of Sass, such as to use an older version that supports some deprecated features used in the project. This can be done as in Listing 2-7.

Listing 2-7. Command for Uninstalling Sass

```
gem uninstall sass --version versionnumber
```

An Alternative to the Command Line

Besides The terminal method, there are GUI applications that will run and compile Sass, for people who are scared to operate or have no prior experience using terminals. There are free as well as paid variants of such apps for various platforms. Some of these are as follows

- Codekit (Paid) (available for Mac only)
- Compass (Paid) (available for Mac, Windows, and Linux)
- Prepros (Paid) (available for Mac, Windows, and Linux)
- Mixtures (Free) (available for Mac only)
- Scout (open source) (available for Mac, Windows, and Linux)
- Koala (Free) (available for Mac, Windows, and Linux)

Compiling the sass File

Once you have installed Sass, you can start coding and compiling. In order to do so, you must specify which file Sass should watch. This can be done using the command shown in Listing 2-8.

Listing 2-8. Sass Command to Watch and Compile a File

```
sass --watch style.scss:style.css
```

The command shown in Listing 2-8 watches the .scss files for any changes. Whenever you modify and save the .scss file, Sass will compile and generate the output .css file. Thus the code given in Listing 2-8 can be broken down in following manner:

- `sass` (main component that indicates that this is a Sass command)
- `--watch` (action this command is supposed to perform)
- `style.scss:style.css` (input and output file separated by colon)

You can find out more about the command options by typing the command shown in Listing 2-9 in the terminal.

Listing 2-9. Command for Accessing Sass Documentation

```
sass --help
```

Avoiding the Command Line with Apps: Using Scout

Scout is a free app built using Adobe air and it can be downloaded from `http://mhs.github.io/scout-app/`. Open the app and click the plus icon at the bottom-left corner to add a project. Figure 2-2 shows the UI of the Scout app.

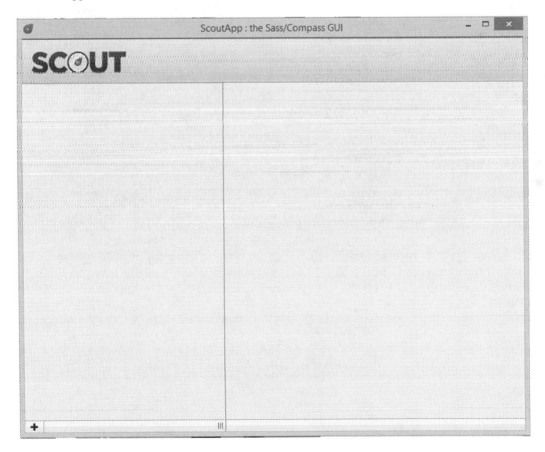

Figure 2-2. *Scout app interface; to get started, you need to click on the bottom-left plus icon*

After you click the plus icon, you will see the interface shown in Figure 2-3.

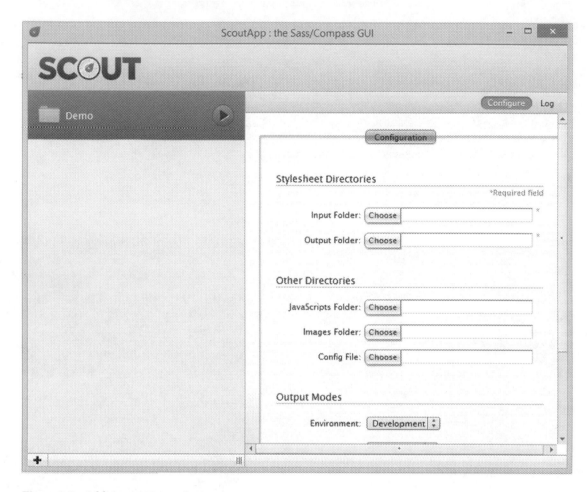

Figure 2-3. *Adding a project to Scout*

As you can see, there are various parameters that you can configure, including stylesheet directories, JavaScript, and images directories. You can also provide specific config files for Sass compilation in the Config File field. Note the Output Modes option. If you leave it as is, you get optimized but readable code. No minification is performed.

You can set various output styles by which output can be further compressed and minified. However, in this case, you will be using the first two fields where you specify the stylesheet input and output folders.

Once you set your required fields, you can initiate a Scout project by clicking the Start button next to the project name. You will then see the screen shown in Figure 2-4.

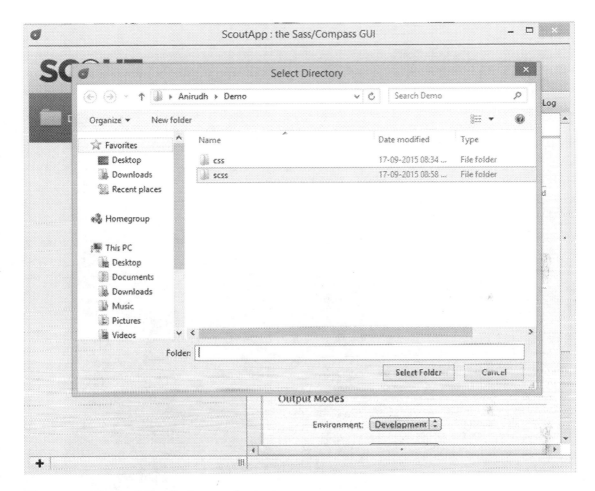

Figure 2-4. *Selecting folders for Input and output*

Scout watches for all the changes that take place and compiles them to appropriate CSS (see Figure 2-5). If there are syntax issues, the user will be notified immediately. You can then minimize the app and continue your development.

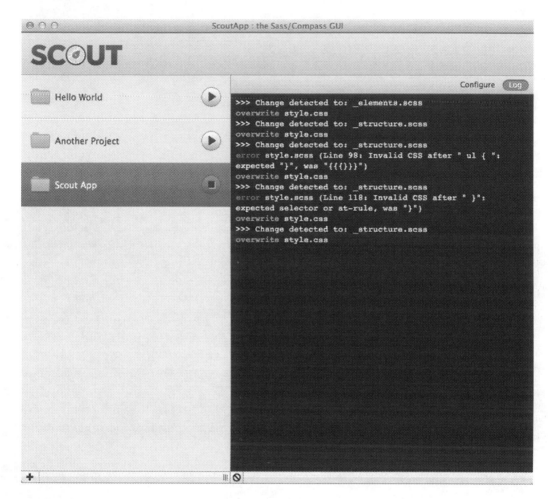

Figure 2-5. *Scout is initiated and watching a project*

Automating Workflow

Like Scout, there are many free tools available to speed up the frontend development. If you want to automate your development further and you are not scared to play with command line, take a look at Yeoman (http://yeoman.io/). See Figure 2-6. This does more than just compile Sass. It is a complete build system that optimizes images, refreshes the browser, etc. Some of the core features it provides are

- *Scaffolding* (As per wiki: "Scaffolding is a technique supported by some model-view-controller frameworks, in which the programmer can specify how the application database may be used. The compiler or framework uses this specification, together with pre-defined code templates, to generate the final code that the application can use to create, read, update and delete database entries, effectively treating the templates as a "scaffold" on which to build a more powerful application. It is usually used by company to for creating as a web-base program. [sic]"

- Build system to generate builds with compressed/compiled code.

- Package manager that will automatically get all the required libraries.

Another such known automation tool is Bower (http://bower.io/).

Figure 2-6. *Go to Yeoman.io to get the Yeoman framework*

Variables

Like other programming languages, variables are used to associate values to a name that is available for reuse across the code. So you end up referring to a name instead of cloning values. In Sass, you can store color, typographic info, and so on, which are reusable. You use $ symbol to create a variable in Sass, as shown in Listing 2-10.

Listing 2-10. Creating Variables in Sass

```
$fontColor:#666;

body{
        color:$fontColor;
}
```

When this Sass code is compiled to normal CSS, $fontColor within the style definition of body gets replaced with the actual value.

Variables, when declared outside any style declaration, are globally accessible. If they are declared inside any specific selector, they will be available only to that specific selector. Take a look at the example in Listing 2-11.

Listing 2-11. Code Demonstrating Scope of Variable

```
body{
  $fontColor:#666;
  color:$fontColor;
}
p{
  color:$fontColor;
}
```

This code will give this error:

```
Undefined variable: "$fontColor".
```

This is because $fontColor is declared inside the style block for the body tag.

Variables can be combined with parts of style rules to make a single style rule. In such an implementation, the variable is replaced by its actual value. This is demonstrated in Listing 2-12.

Listing 2-12. Code Combining Parts of CSS Rules with Variables

```
$border-color: #000;
.containerBlock {
  border: 2px $border-color solid;
}
```

It is possible to create a variable from another variable. This can be done as shown in Listing 2-13.

Listing 2-13. Declaring One Variable from Another Variable

```
$border-color: #000;
$borderDeclaration: 2px $border-color solid;
.containerBlock {
  border:$borderDeclaration;
}
```

Sass allows you to use underscores and hyphens interchangeably in your code. Thus, the code shown in Listing 2-14 will be valid and won't produce an error.

Listing 2-14. Demo Showing the Interchangable Use of Underscores and Hyphens

```
$color-positive: #0f0;
.note {
color: $color_positive;
}
```

Data Types

Sass supports various data types:

- Numbers (e.g., 2.0,15,12px)
- Strings (e.g., "foo",bar)
- Colors (e.g., #f00, rgb(255,255,150))
- Boolean (e.g., true, false)
- Comma- or space-separated values (e.g., 10px 20px, 'Tahoma','Arial',san-serif)

Sass also supports css !important declarations.

Default Values for Variables

Variables can be given default values that will come into action if they are not assigned any specific value. This comes handy when you want to use a default value across your code and modify it only in certain situations, as shown in Listings 2-15 and 2-16.

Listing 2-15. Example of Default Values

```
$borderRadius: 5px !default;
```

Listing 2-16. Example of a Default Value Being Ignored When a Value Is Specified Explicitly

```
$borderRadius:10px;
.notArea{
        Border-radius:$borderRadius;
}
```

Listing 2-17. Output of Listing 2-16

```
.notArea{
        Border-radius:10px;
}
```

If the code in Listing 2-16 runs without explicitly specifying the value for borderRadius, it will choose go ahead with default value. Output will thus be as shown in Listing 2-18.

Listing 2-18. Output of Listing 2-16 Without Explicitly Defining a Value for borderRadius

```
.notArea{
        Border-radius:5px;
}
```

Nesting Styles in Sass

While writing CSS, you have to repeat the selectors to assign style rules for elements placed under some elements. The code shown in Listing 2-19 is a common example of selector repetition.

Listing 2-19. Code Repetition in CSS

```
.article .h1 {
  font-weight: bold;
}

.article p {
  line-height: 1em;
}

.article img {
  float: left;
}
```

In Sass, you can avoid this code repetition by nesting CSS selectors. Thus, the code in Listing 2-19, rewritten in Sass, would look like Listing 2-20.

Listing 2-20. Sass Version of the Code in Listing 2-19

```
.article{
  .h1{
    font-weight:bold;
  }
  p{
    line-height:1em;
  }
  img{
    float:left;
  }
}
```

This approach not only eliminates code repetition, it also makes the code more readable. Nesting can be done with groups of selectors as well. This is shown in Listing 2-21.

Listing 2-21. Nesting a Group of Selectors

```
.article{
  p,section{
    line-height:1em;
  }
}
```

Listing 2-22. Output of Listing 2-21

```
.article p, .article section {
  line-height: 1em;
}
```

Referencing a Parent Selector: &

When nesting styles in Sass, there are many occasions where you might need to refer to the parent selector. For example, if you want to write a style for a hover state of an element, you can refer to the parent element by prefixing the & selector, as shown in Listing 2-23.

Listing 2-23. Using & to Refer to the Parent Selector

```
a {
        text-decoration:none;
        &:hover {
                text-decoration.underline;
        }
}
```

When this code is compiled, & is replaced with the parent selector. The compiled output is shown in Listing 2-24.

Listing 2-24. Output of Listing 2-23

```
a {
        text-decoration:none;
}
a:hover{
        text-decoration:underline;
}
```

Another feature of & is that it resolves the parent selector regardless of any depth in nesting. Consider the code in Listing 2-25.

Listing 2-25. & Is Nested Two Levels Below in the Style Declaration

```
#contentArea {
      font-size:1em;
      a#referenceLinkContainer{
              background:#CCC;
              &:hover{
                      border:1px solid #000;
              }
      }
}
```

The output is shown in Listing 2-26.

Listing 2-26. Compiled output of Listing 2-25

```
#contentArea{ font-size: 1em;}
#contentArea a#referenceLinkContainer{background: #CCC;}
#contentArea a#referenceLinkContainer:hover{border:1px solid #000;}
```

Using Combinators in Your SCSS

Combinator selectors— +, >, and ~ —are used to combine selectors. They tell the browser which elements are in context.

The > is also known as the *child combinator*. It's used to select the immediate child of the parent. In the previous example, it would select the immediate h1 of section. It will not target any h1's that have been nested inside a child element. See Listing 2-27.

Listing 2-27. Example of Using a Combinator in CSS

```
.article{
  section > h1{
    line-height:1em;
  }
}
```

The + is also known as the *adjacent combinator*. It's used to select the next element at the same level. It would not check the parent element's children. It's shown in Listings 2-28 and 2-29.

Listing 2-28. HTML Markup to Demonstrate an Adjacent Combinator

```
<section>
      <article>
              <p>This is a child paragraph</p>
      </article>
      <p>This is an adjacent paragraph</p>
      <article>
              <p>This is a child paragraph</p>
      </article>
</section>
```

Listing 2-29. CSS Demonstrating an Adjacent Combinator

```
Article + p{
        Color: #F00;
}
```

In the code shown in Listing 2-29, the rule will apply to any p tag that is after the article tag and not ones that are inside the article tags.

The ~ is called the *general sibling* combinator. It will select every article that comes after another article, regardless of what elements are between them. See Listing 2-30.

Listing 2-30. CSS Demonstrating the General Sibling Combinator

```
Article ~ article{
        Color: #F00;
}
```

Comments

Like other programming languages, Sass supports single-line and multiline comments. Single-line comments are created by prefixing them with //. Multiline comments are enclosed within /**/. Listing 2-31 shows some examples.

Listing 2-31. Comment Examples

```
// This is Single line comment
/* This is a
Multi line comment */
```

When the Sass file is compiled, multiline comments are retained while single-line comments are removed.

Nesting Properties

Like nested rules, Sass also allows nesting of properties. For example, consider the properties like font-family, font-size, and font-weight. These all come under the font namespace.

In Sass, you can nest properties that come under the same namespace, as shown in Listing 2-32.

Listing 2-32. Nesting Properties

```
.content{
font: {
        family: 'Tahoma';
        size: 13px;
        weight: bold;
        }
}
```

This code is compiled as shown in Listing 2-33.

Listing 2-33. Output of Listing 2-32

```
.content{
       font-family: 'Tahoma';
       font-size: 13px;
       font-weight: bold;
}
```

Interpolation

If you want to build your selectors or properties dynamically, interpolation is the thing you need. This comes handy when you want use loops to generate styles. For example, you have an array containing names of social network icons. You can use loop with interpolation to generate such styles. It can be used in a simple situation where you want use a value stored in a variable in a class name, as demonstrated in Listing 2-34.

Interpolation is done using the #{} syntax.

Listing 2-34. Example Showing Interpolation

```
$innerContainerClass: container;
.left .#{$innerContainerClass} {
       width:50%;
       display:inline-block;
}
```

Listing 2-35. Output of Listing 2-34

```
.left .container{
       width:50%;
       display:inline-block;
}
```

Placeholder Selectors

Placeholder selectors are special types of selectors that look similar to normal IDs or class selectors, but are prefixed by % instead of # or .. Placeholders differ from other selectors in that they are not rendered in the final output .css file.

Placeholder selectors (see Listing 2-36) are used to extend certain sets of styles without rendering that set in the final output. You will see its implementation the next chapter when you look at @extend.

Listing 2-36. Example of a Placeholder Selector

```
%importantText{
       Color:red;
       Font-weight:bold;
}

.notice{
       @extend %importantText;
}
```

Listing 2-37. Output of Listing 2-36, where %importantText Has Been Rendered

```
.notice {
  Color: red;
  Font-weight: bold;
}
```

Logical Capabilities of Sass

Sass not only makes writing CSS easy and maintainable by incorporating the DRY principle, but it also adds capabilities such as logic and calculations, which were missing in core CSS. With Sass, you can perform math calculations, perform some operations on the basis of some condition, or do some looping. Let's look into these aspects in more detail.

Mathematical Operations in Sass

Sass supports addition, subtraction, multiplication, and division.

Addition

Addition can be done as shown in Listing 2-38.

Listing 2-38. Example Showing Addition

```
.container{ width: 20%+80%;}
```

Note that mathematical operations can occur only with same type of operands. In other words, you cannot perform mathematical operations between pixel and percentage.

Subtraction

Subtraction can be done as shown in Listing 2-39.

Listing 2-39. Example Showing Subtraction

```
.container{ width: 80%-40%;}
```

Multiplication

Multiplication can be done as shown in Listing 2-40.

Listing 2-40. Example showing Multiplication

```
.container{ width: 80%*40%;}
```

Division

Division can be done as shown in Listing 2-41.

Listing 2-41. Example showing Division

```
.container{ width: 80%/40%;}
```

Parentheses

In Sass, parentheses are used to manipulate the order of execution, as shown in Listing 2-42.

Listing 2-42. Parentheses in Action

```
.leftSide{
        Font-size:1em + (.2em*2);
}
```

Listing 2-43. Output of Listing 2-42

```
.leftSide{
        Font-size:1.4em;
}
```

Calculations Using Variables

Calculations can be performed with variables as well. Check out Listing 2-44.

Listing 2-44. Example of Performing Calculations Using Variables

```
$container:100%;
$contentArea:50%;
$gutter:10%;
.sidebar{
  width: $container - ($contentArea+$gutter);
}
```

Control Directives

Sass provides control directives for including styles or bringing some variations in styles based on some condition.

Control directives are complex and aren't typically used on a daily basis. They are mainly used in mixins in order to make them flexible. This is commonly seen in mixins within libraries like Compass, which is covered in coming chapters.

@if

This control directive takes an expression and applies the associated style if the expression evaluates to something other than false or null, as shown in Listing 2-45.

Listing 2-45. Example of Using @if

```
$isVisible : true !default;
.container{
  @if $isVisible{
    display: block;
  }
  @else{
    display: none;
  }
}
```

In the previous code, $isVisible is evaluated inside .container and, depending on the result, a style is applied.

Listing 2-46. Output of Listing 2-45

```
.container {
  display: block;
}
```

@if can be combined with one or more @else if statements and one @else statement. Listing 2-47 shows an example where the background color is applied in hex code based on the color specified in the text form.

Listing 2-47. Combination of @if, @else if, and @else

```
$blockColor: green;
.container {
  @if $blockColor == red {
    background-color: #f00;
  } @else if $blockColor == green {
    background-color: #0f0;
  } @else if $blockColor == blue {
    background-color: #00f;
  } @else {
    background-color: #000;
  }
}
```

Listing 2-48. Combination of @if, @else if, and @else

```
.container {
  background-color: #0f0;
}
```

@for

The @for directive is used to output styles by means of looping. Using the @for loop, you can adjust styles based on the value of the counter. There are two variations of this:

- Using through ($counter from <start_value> through <end_value>)

- Using to ($counter from <start_value> to <end_value>)

When <start_value> is greater than <end_value>, the counter will decrement. The main difference between through and to is that the former one includes the <end_value> while the latter one doesn't. See Listings 2-49 through 2-52.

Listing 2-49. Example of Using @for with through

```
@for $size from 1 through 3 {
  .header-#{$size} { font-size: 2em * $size; }
}
```

Listing 2-50. Output of Listing 2-49

```
.header-1 {
  font-size: 2em;
}

.header-2 {
  font-size: 4em;
}

.header-3 {
  font-size: 6em;
}
```

Listing 2-51. Example of Using @for with to

```
@for $size from 1 to 3 {
  .header-#{$size} { font-size: 2em * $size; }
}
```

Listing 2-52. Output of Listing 2-51

```
.header-1 {
  font-size: 2em;
}

.header-2 {
  font-size: 4em;
}
```

@each

The @each directive is another looping directive like @for, except that instead of using counters, you provide a list that determines which operation is performed.

Consider an example where you're building styles for social icons, as shown in Listing 2-53. You loop an array that contains the names of the social icons and, using interpolation, you generate style classes with their names and background images.

Listing 2-53. Example Demonstrating the @each Implementation

```
$socials: twitter linkedin pinterest;
@each $social in $socials {
  .#{$social} {
    background-image: url(/images/icons/#{$social}.png);
    width:16px;height:16px;
  }
}
```

Listing 2-54. Output of Listing 2-53

```
.twitter {
  background-image: url(/images/icons/twitter.png);
  width: 16px;
  height: 16px;
}

.linkedin {
  background-image: url(/images/icons/linkedin.png);
  width: 16px;
  height: 16px;
}

.pinterest {
  background-image: url(/images/icons/pinterest.png);
  width: 16px;
  height: 16px;
}
```

It is possible to have multiple variables and list them in @each, as shown in Listing 2-55. In this example, you are using two variables as one element in a loop. A pair of $notification and $color is treated as a single loop entity and it's evaluated and the styles are generated accordingly.

Listing 2-55. An Example Demonstrating an @each Implementation Using Multiple Lists

```
@each $notification, $color in (success, green),(warning, amber),(error,red) {
  .#{$notification}-icon {
    background-color: $color;
  }
}
```

Listing 2-56. Output of Listing 2-55

```
.success-icon {
  background-color: green;
}

.warning-icon {
  background-color: amber;
}

.error-icon {
  background-color: red;
}
```

@while

The @while directive iterates until the condition given is not met and outputs the styles nested inside the body of the while loop. Listing 2-57 shows an example that builds the column layout for a responsive design. It's building a four-column grid using a while loop.

Listing 2-57. Example Demonstrating @while

```
$col: 4;
@while $col > 0 {
  .cols-#{$col} {
    width: 100% / $col;
  }
  $col: $col - 1;
}
```

Listing 2-58. Output of Listing 2-57

```
.cols-4 {
  width: 25%;
}

.cols-3 {
  width: 33.33333%;
}

.cols-2 {
  width: 50%;
}

.cols-1 {
  width: 100%;
}
```

Summary

This chapter introduced the fundamental components of Sass. In the next chapter, you will be diving in to advanced aspects of Sass, such as creating mixins and extending existing styles.

CHAPTER 3

■ ■ ■

Advanced Sass

In the previous chapter, you looked into the installation procedure and essential components needed to work with Sass. In this chapter, you will look into the more advanced concepts of Sass.

This chapter explores the following aspects of Sass:

- @import
- @media
- @extend
- @at-root
- Mixin directives
- Function directives
- Output style
- Building your own grid system

@import

Sass also supports importing features similar to what is available in native CSS. But unlike CSS, which downloads CSS when an @import is encountered, Sass and SCSS files imported using the SASS @import rules will be merged and output as a single file after compilation.

When you specify Sass import in a file, it looks into the current directory. Additional search paths can be specified using the load_paths option. By default it takes a file name.

Listing 3-1. Example of @import

```
@import "main"
```
@import can be used for importing multiple files as well.

Listing 3-2. Example of @import for Getting Multiple Files

```
@import "main", "mobile"
```

This behavior is shown in Figure 3-1.

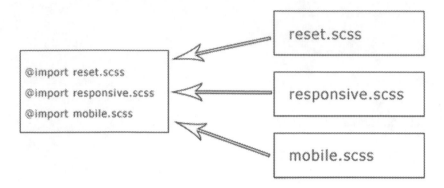

Figure 3-1. *Visual representation of how @import works in Sass*

Partials

Let's say you have some reusable chunk of Sass code that you want to import but don't want to see it in the final output file. You can use partials to achieve this result. Partials come in handy for segregating the style code in various files for better organization.

Let's say you have a Sass file containing information regarding typography like font size and weights with the name typography.scss. To make this file partial, you need to prefix it with an underscore. So the file name would be _typography.scss. The underscore tells the Sass compiler that the specified file is a partial and need not be compiled into complete CSS.

This makes managing style code in the project easier as the project grows, by sorting code into logical chunks.

Thus continuing with example from previous paragraph, after renaming the file _typography.scss, you can import it in the code with a simple @import typography statement.

Nested @import

Imports can also be used for importing code snippets within style rules. Using @import, you can also import CSS rules.

Let's take an example where you have two files—parent.scss and file2.scss. Say you want to import the content of parent.scss into file2.scss. You could do so as shown in Listing 3-3.

Listing 3-3. Example of @import for Importing Style: Content of _parent.scss

```
.parent{
     Background-color:#CCC;
}
```

Listing 3-4. Example of @import for Importing Style: Content of file2.scss

```
.child{
     @import "parent";
}
```

When the code shown in Listing 3-4 is executed, you get the output shown in Listing 3-5.

Listing 3-5. Output of Listing 3-4

```
.child .parent{
        Background-color:#CCC;
}
```

Thus when you apply `import` within a style rule, all the imported rules will be nested inside that specific rule. The result of this will be same as if the styles were nested inside that specific selector.

Plain CSS Imports

In addition to its own style of `import`, Sass also supports the CSS style `@import`. There are two factors that cause such a behavior to be triggered. These are as follows:

- URL/path of the file to be imported ends with a `.css` extension
- URL/path of the file to be imported begins with `http(s)://`

Thus, you cannot import plain CSS directly in Sass. However, there is a workaround for this. Since Sass is compatible with CSS, you can simply change the extension of the file from `.css` to `.scss` and import it.

@media

Media queries are the most essential part of today's web design process. With media queries, you can customize your web app based on things like viewport width, viewport height, device width, device height, and orientation.

Normally, a developer building a web page would first write "normal" styles and then write media queries at the end. This would work fine for stylesheets with few lines of code; however, it will be nightmare to manage when the code increases to thousands of lines.

Sass provides something much easier. `@media` is used to write media queries similar to CSS. However, it has an added feature that it can be nested within a style rule. Sass will automatically build a media queries declaration and put respective styles inside it, as shown in Listing 3-6.

Listing 3-6. @media Inside Sass

```
#container{
        Width:960px;
        @media screen and (min-width:500px){
                Width:100%;}
}
```

Listing 3-7. Output of Listing 3-6

```
#container {
  Width: 960px;
}

@media screen and (min-width: 500px) {
  #container {
    Width: 100%;
  }
}
```

Now you might be wondering why we would use a preprocessor for writing a media query instead of using the conventional CSS method. One of the advantages is code readability. By using the Sass way of integrating the media query, the code is very easy to understand.

Sass also allows nesting of media queries for building complex media queries. Consider the example in Listing 3-8, where we have nested media queries for different width inside the #container. This makes the code easy to understand and far more readable.

Listing 3-8. Nesting of Media Queries

```
@media screen {
  #container {
    @media (min-width:500px) {
      width: 500px;
    }
    @media (min-width:700px) {
      width: 700px;
    }
  }
}
```

Listing 3-9. Ouput of Listing 3-8

```
@media screen and (min-width: 500px) {
  #container {
    width: 500px;
  }
}

@media screen and (min-width: 700px) {
  #container {
    width: 700px;
  }
}
```

Going further, you can create a partial with media queries inside them and then include them wherever needed.

With Sass, you can also include media queries inline. Consider an example where you want a container to have different width on different viewport sizes. This can be achieved as demonstrated in Listing 3-10.

Listing 3-10. Inline Media Queries

```
$color1:#CCC;
.color {
  color: $color1;
  @include setQuery(sm) {
    width: 80%;
  }
  @include setQuery(md) {
    width: 70%;
  }
  @include setQuery(lg) {
    width: 60%;
  }
}
```

Yet another advantage of writing media queries using Sass is that you can assign breakpoints for media queries to variables. Then these variables can be used in media queries. This is demonstrated in Listing 3-11, which is a more elaborate version of the previous example.

Listing 3-11. Using Variables for Assigning Breakpoint

```
$color1:#CCC;
$sm:320px;
$md:720px;
$lg:1280px;
@mixin setQuery($type){
  @if $type == sm {
    @media only screen and (min-width: $sm) and (max-width: $md - 1) {
      @content;
    }
  }
  @else if $type == md {
    @media only screen and (min-width: $md) and (max-width: $lg - 1) {
      @content;
    }
  }
  @else if $type == lg {
    @media only screen and (min-width: $lg){
      @content
    }
  }
}
.container {
  color: $color1;
  @include setQuery(sm) {
    width: 80%;
  }
  @include setQuery(md) {
    width: 70%;
  }
  @include setQuery(lg) {
    width: 60%;
  }
}
```

The previous code example stored width values in variables. Then, on the basis of which variable we pass as the parameter to the mixin (which is like a function used to inject reusable style with computation if needed, a concept that's covered later in the chapter), the media query is generated and injected. The output of the previous code is as shown in Listing 3-12.

Listing 3-12. Output of Listing 3-11

```
.container {
  color: #CCC;
}

@media only screen and (min-width: 320px) and (max-width: 719px) {
  .container {
    width: 80%;
  }
}

@media only screen and (min-width: 720px) and (max-width: 1279px) {
  .container {
    width: 70%;
  }
}

@media only screen and (min-width: 1280px) {
  .container {
    width: 60%;
  }
}
```

@extend

When writing CSS, one situation we might come across often is where one class needs to have all the style rules of another, plus its own style. Writing this using simple CSS would require repeating the code. Using Sass, you can inherit these required styles using @extend.

@extend is known as a selector inheritance. In selector inheritance, Sass inherits all the styles defined in another selector. Consider the example shown in Listing 3-13, where .notification is inherited in .success.

Listing 3-13. An Example of Using @extend

```
.notification{
  border-radius:5px;
  padding:5px;
}

.success{
  @extend .notification;
  background-color:#0F0;
}
```

Listing 3-14. Output of Listing 3-13

```
.notification, .success {
  border-radius: 5px;
  padding: 5px;
}
```

```
.success {
  background-color: #0F0;
}
```

There are some disadvantages of using @extend. For one, the result of extending may sometimes be unpredictable in a large file where the extended CSS selector is present multiple times. This could result in undesirable output.

Another issue with using @extend is that it cannot be used inside @media declarations.

@extend is also not as flexible as using mixins, as it cannot accept arguments.

It is possible to create a single selector by extending multiple selectors, as shown in Listing 3-15.

Listing 3-15. Extending from Multiple Selectors

```
.notification {
        border-radius: 5px;
        padding: 5px;
}
.errorLooks{
      Color:#F00;
      Background-color:rgba(255,0,0,0.5);
}
.error {
        @extend .notification;
        @extend .errorLooks;
}
```

Listing 3-16. Output of Listing 3-15

```
.notification, .error {
  border-radius: 5px;
  padding: 5px;
}

.errorLooks, .error {
  Color: #F00;
  Background-color: rgba(255, 0, 0, 0.5);
}
```

You can also perform chaining by extending the selectors in the next selector, as shown in Listing 3-17.

Listing 3-17. Chaining Within extend

```
.notification {
        border-radius: 5px;
        padding: 5px;
}
.errorLooks{
  @extend .notification;
      Color:#F00;
      Background-color:rgba(255,0,0,0.5);
}
.error {
  @extend .errorLooks;
}
```

Listing 3-18. Output of Listing 3-17

```
.notification, .errorLooks, .error {
  border-radius: 5px;
  padding: 5px;
}

.errorLooks, .error {
  Color: #F00;
  Background-color: rgba(255, 0, 0, 0.5);
}
```

@extend Behind the Scenes

Inheritance isn't as simple as it seems. Understanding how extending works will give you insight into how selectors are inherited and thus will give you the ability to anticipate the output.

Let's take example used in previous section. The principle behind @extend is that if .error extends .notification, every instance of .error in the final stylesheet will be replaced with .notification, .error. There are two things regarding @extend that you should keep in mind:

- Inheritance generates comparatively less CSS than mixins, which does a somewhat similar thing. It only adds the selector in a comma-separated list and does not clone the properties.

- Cascading applies to inheritance similarly to how it does in normal CSS. When two rules with different values apply to the same element, cascading decides which rule will be applied. Thus the last rule is always applied.

When to Use Selector Inheritance

Suppose you are developing a web page and writing style rules and you find that one of your classes (.errorLooks) is a more specific version of another (.notification). How will you go about writing the style rule?

- You could replicate the same style rules in both the classes. However, this would result in lot of duplicate code and would go against the DRY principle.

- You could apply styles to group of selectors (.notification, .error). This is good, but over time will increase the complexity of your style code.

- You could use @extend provided by Sass and allow .error inherit from .notification. This makes the code far more readable and easier to understand.

Placeholder Selectors

While using Sass, you might come across situations where you want to write classes that you want to extend into other classes but don't want it to be rendered into the final compiled CSS file. For example, you want to use a certain class containing code for rounded edges or margins that's not useful independently.

This can be achieved in Sass with something known as placeholder selector, which is rendered by prefixing the class name with %—for example %notification.

Listing 3-19. Example of @extend Selectors

```
%notification {
        border-radius: 5px;
        padding: 5px;
}
.errorLooks{
  @extend %notification;
}
```

Listing 3-20. Output of Listing 3-19

```
.errorLooks {
  border-radius: 5px;
  padding: 5px;
}
```

As you see in Listing 3-20, the notification extend class has not been rendered in the final output.

Do More with @extend

Classes are not the only things that can be extended. It is also possible to extend complex elements like a:hover, .notification, and .error, as shown in Listing 3-21.

Listing 3-21. Example Demonstrating Extending a Complex Element

```
a{
  color:#F00;
  &:hover{
    font-weight:bold;
  }
}
.notification{
        @extend a:hover ;
}
```

It is also possible to create multiple rules by extending multiple CSS classes in one selector, as shown in Listing 3-22.

Listing 3-22. Example Demonstrating Extending Multiple Classes

```
.notification{
        Border-radius:50%;
}
.strongText{
        Font-weight:bold;
}
.error{
        @extend .notification;
        @extend .strongText;
        Color:#F00;
}
```

This code will give the output shown in Listing 3-23.

Listing 3-23. Output of Listing 3-22

```
.notification, .error {
  Border-radius: 50%;
}

.strongText, .error {
  Font-weight: bold;
}

.error {
  Color: #F00;
}
```

It is also possible to chain the selectors while extending; that is, extending one selector that already extends another selector. Here is the modified code of Listing 3-24 to demonstrate this phenomenon.

Listing 3-24. Example Demonstrating Chaining extends

```
.notification{
      Border-radius:50%;
}
.strongText{
  @extend .notification;
      Font-weight:bold;
}
.error{
      @extend .strongText;
      Color:#F00;
}
```

The output of this code will be same as shown in Listing 3-23.

There might be situations where you want @extend to be ignored if the extended selector has as error or is not present. You can use the !optional flag in that case. This will prevent @extend from producing results. This is demonstrated in Listing 3-25.

Listing 3-25. Example Showing !optional

```
.success{
  @extend .lightText !optional;
}
```

@at-root

The Sass @at-root directive causes the rules inside it to be rendered at the document root level, regardless of where they are nested. See Listing 3-26.

Listing 3-26. Example of @at-root

```
.notification {
        border-radius: 5px;
        padding: 5px;
}
.errorLooks{
  @extend .notification;
  @at-root{
    .icon{
      border-radius:50%;
    }
  }
}
```

In this example, `.icon` is nested in the `errorLooks`. This code when compiled will give the result shown in Listing 3-27.

Listing 3-27. Output of Listing 3-26

```
.notification, .errorLooks {
  border-radius: 5px;
  padding: 5px;
}

.icon {
  border-radius: 50%;
}
```

Note that the content in `@at-root` will appear after the rules within which it was nested.

You might be thinking, "When could I use this myself?"

Well, with `@at-root`, your code would be more readable and manageable. Consider the example shown in Listing 3-28.

Listing 3-28. Example of Implementing @at-root

```
.productImage {
  height: 150px;
  width: 150px;

  @at-root {
    @keyframes panimate {
      0% { transform: scale(1.0); }
      25% { transform: scale(1.1); }
      50% { transform: scale(1.2); }
      75% { transform: scale(1.1); }
      100% { transform: scale(1.0); }
    }
  }
  &:hover {
    animation: panimate .8s infinite;
  }
}
```

In this example, you can see that putting an animation declaration that will be used for this specific element inside the definition with @at-root increases the overall code readability.

Listing 3-29. Output of Listing 3-28

```
.productImage {
  height: 150px;
  width: 150px;
}

@keyframes panimate {
  0% {
    transform: scale(1);
  }
  25% {
    transform: scale(1.1);
  }
  50% {
    transform: scale(1.2);
  }
  75% {
    transform: scale(1.1);
  }
  100% {
    transform: scale(1);
  }
}

.productImage:hover {
  animation: panimate 0.8s infinite;
}
```

Mixin Directives

As your CSS grows, you'll come across situations where you need to replicate entire chunk of styles as-is or with slight variations.

Mixins, declared using @mixin, are used to create reusable style code that can be used across the entire stylesheet. Mixins can contain full CSS rules. Mixins can take arguments, which makes them flexible.

Mixins are defined using the @mixin directive followed by the name of the mixin and optional argument and block containing code, as shown in Listing 3-30.

Listing 3-30. Example of a Mixin

```
@mixin roundedEdges($radius:5px) {
  -webkit-border-radius: $radius;
    -moz-border-radius: $radius;
     -ms-border-radius: $radius;
        border-radius: $radius;
}
.container {@include roundedEdges(10px);}
```

This example shows a mixin that generates code for rounded edges, which accepts a single parameter whose default value is set to 5px if it's not provided.

Listing 3-31. Output of Listing 3-30

```
.container {
  -webkit-border-radius: 10px;
  -moz-border-radius: 10px;
  -ms-border-radius: 10px;
  border-radius: 10px;
}
```

This example shows how the mixins are defined and included. The mixins are defined using @mixin. They are included using @include. In this example, we have also provided an argument with its default value.

You can also create compounded mixins, by including other mixins, as shown in Listing 3-32.

Listing 3-32. Example of a Compound Mixin

```
@mixin success {
  @include notification;
  @include successTheme;
}
```

Mixin arguments are written in variable format, separated by commas if more than one argument is there. These arguments can have default values that will be used if no value is provided as an argument.

Listing 3-33. Passing a Block of Code as an Argument to a Mixin

```
@mixin clearFix {
  &:after {
    @content;
  }
}

.btn {
  display: inline-block;
  @include clearFix {
    clear:both;
  }
}
```

Listing 3-34. Output of Listing 3-33

```
.btn {
  display: inline-block;
}

.btn:after {
  clear: both;
}
```

Mixins versus Classes

Mixins make reusing styles in a stylesheet very easy. Any piece of style code that's repeated is a good candidate for a mixin. For example, a group of properties that make sense to set together like border radius, background gradient, and so on, would be a good mixin.

Mixins are very similar to CSS classes. Both let you store chunks of style. The most important difference between these two is that classes are meant to be used in your HTML, whereas mixins are used to create reusable chunks to use within stylesheets.

Hence, the classes should have a meaningful name that properly identifies the element. Mixins names should be related to the functionality they provide.

Mixins with CSS Selectors

Mixins can contain CSS selectors in addition to properties. This is demonstrated in Listing 3-35.

Listing 3-35. CSS Selectors Within a Mixin

```
@mixin importantInfo {
  font-weight:strong;
  li {
    margin: 0px 5px;
  }
}

.notfication{
  border-radius:35%;
  @include importantInfo;
}
```

This example creates a mixin named importantInfo, which contains its own style rule plus the CSS selector li with its own rule. This is included in the notification class. The result of this code is shown in Listing 3-36.

Listing 3-36. Output of Listing 3-35

```
.notfication {
  border-radius: 35%;
  font-weight:strong;
}

.notfication li {
  margin: 0px 5px;
}
```

Arguments to Mixins

Mixins in Sass can accept arguments that are provided while calling that mixin. This helps the mixin provide different behaviors, depending on arguments provided and thus make it useful for a wide range of scenarios.

Arguments are passed as comma-separated lists of variables, inside parentheses, after the name of the mixin. This is demonstrated in Listing 3-37.

Listing 3-37. Passing Arguments in Mixins

```
@mixin fancyBorder($fbColor, $fbWidth) {
  border-color: $fbColor;
  border-width: $fbWidth;
  border-style: dashed;
}

.specialNote{
  @include fancyBorder(#000,2px)
}
```

This example includes the mixin named fancyBorder, which takes two arguments: borderColor and borderWidth. The output of this is shown in Listing 3-38.

Listing 3-38. Output of Listing 3-37

```
.specialNote {
  border-color: #000;
  border-width: 2px;
  border-style: dashed;
}
```

Mixins can also assume default values for their arguments. Thus, when you don't pass any value to the mixin, it will assume the default values. This can be demonstrated by modifying the code in Listing 3-39.

Listing 3-39. Example Demonstrating Default Variables

```
@mixin fancyBorder($fbColor:#000, $fbWidth:2px) {
  Border-color: $fbColor;
  Border-width: $fbWidth;
  Border-style: dashed;
}

.specialNote{
  @include fancyBorder;
}
```

Mixins also allow you to pass keyword arguments. This makes mixins even more flexible by allowing arguments to be passed in any order. This is shown in Listing 3-40.

Listing 3-40. Keyword Argument Example

```
.specialNote{
  @include fancyBorder($borderColor:#00F, $borderWidth:1px)
}
```

You can make mixins even more flexible by allowing them to deal with an unknown number of variables. Sass supports variable arguments. These are declared at the end of parameters for mixins/functions that contain all additional arguments in the form of a list. These arguments look like normal arguments, but have additional ... at the end. Listing 3-41 shows a modified version of the previous code, and it passes a variable parameter named fontProp to set the font attribute.

Listing 3-41. Example of a Variable Argument

```
@mixin fancyBorder($borderColor:#000, $borderWidth:2px,$fontProp…) {
  border: {
    color: $borderColor;
    width: $borderWidth;
    style: dashed;
  }
  font:$fontProp;
}

.specialNote{
  @include fancyBorder(#00F, 1px,1px arial,sans-serif)
}
```

Listing 3-42. Output of Listing 3-41

```
.specialNote {
  border-color: #00F;
  border-width: 1px;
  border-style: dashed;
  font: 1px arial, sans-serif;
}
```

Using Content Blocks in Mixins

You can also pass blocks of styles to the mixin, which can be placed in addition to the styles provided by mixins. These styles are added wherever the @content rule is declared. The modified version of the previous example would look as shown in Listing 3-43.

Listing 3-43. Example of Content Block

```
@mixin fancyBorder($borderColor:#000, $borderWidth:2px,$fontProp…) {
  border: {
    color: $borderColor;
    width: $borderWidth;
    style: dashed;
  }
  font:$fontProp;
  @content;
}

.specialNote{
  @include fancyBorder(#00F, 1px,1px arial,sans-serif){
    line-height:0.8em;
  }
}
```

The output of this snippet is shown in Listing 3-44.

Listing 3-44. Output of Listing 3-43

```
.specialNote {
  border-color: #00F;
  border-width: 1px;
  border-style: dashed;
  font: 1px arial, sans-serif;
  line-height: 0.8em;
}
```

Function Directives

Functions in Sass perform specified operations on the provided arguments. The syntax of these functions is similar to CSS functions like rgb(). Unlike CSS functions, Sass functions can have keyword arguments and return values useful for Sass operations.

Sass provides built-in functions that are designed to be widely useful in many different circumstances, like color manipulation, and so on. In addition to that, Sass allows users to define their own functions, similar to defining mixins.

Some of the built-in functions provided by Sass are categorized as follows:

- Numeric functions
- Color functions
- List functions

Numeric Functions

Sass provides a few functions for dealing with numeric values, especially for situations that come up frequently when writing stylesheets with Sass.

Some of these are discussed in the following sections.

abs($number)

This function will return an absolute value of the number, as shown in Listing 3-45.

Listing 3-45. Example Using abs

```
$fontsize:1.1em;
.container{
  // Will use 1.1em
  font-size:abs($fontsize);
}
```

ceil($number)

This function will return a rounded-up value of a number, as shown in Listing 3-46.

Listing 3-46. Example Using ceil

```
$fontsize:1.1em;
.container{
  // Will use 2em
  font-size:ceil($fontsize);
}
```

floor($number)

This function will return a rounded-down value of a number, as shown in Listing 3-47.

Listing 3-47. Example Using floor

```
$fontsize:1.1em;
.container{
  // Will use 1em
  font-size:floor($fontsize);
}
```

percentage($number)

This function will convert the provided number into a percentage and return it. The number provided as the argument should be unitless, i.e., it should not possess a unit as a suffix. See Listing 3-48.

Listing 3-48. Example Using percentage

```
$fontsize:1.1;
.container{
  // Will use 110%
  font-size:percentage($fontsize);
}
```

round($number)

This function will return the nearest round value of the number provided, as shown in Listing 3-49.

Listing 3-49. Example Using round

```
$fontsize:1.1em;
.container{
  // Will use 1em
  font-size:round($fontsize);
}
```

Color Functions

Sass provided various functions for transforming the colors, such as `adjust_color`, `complement`, `greyscale`, `invert`, etc.

Some of these are described in the following sections.

adjust_color($color,...)

This function is used to assign individual properties of colors such as red, green, blue, etc. The properties are specified as keyword arguments and values are added or subtracted from the original value (see Listing 3-50). The following properties of the color can be transformed using this function:

- Red
- Green
- Blue
- Hue
- Lightness
- Alpha

Listing 3-50. Example Showing adjust_color

```
$fontcolor:#900;
.container{
  color:adjust_color($fontcolor,$red:-5);
}
```

complcmcnt($color)

This function returns the complement of the color, as shown in Listing 3-51.

Listing 3-51. Example Showing complement

```
$fontcolor:#FF0000;
.container{
  color:complement($fontcolor);
}
```

The output of the previous code snippet is shown in Listing 3-52.

Listing 3-52. Output of Listing 3-53.

```
.container {
  color: cyan;
}
```

grayscale($color)

This function returns the grayscale version of a color. This is demonstrated in Listing 3-53.

Listing 3-53. Example of grayscale

```
$fontcolor:#FFCC00;
.container{
  color:grayscale($fontcolor);
}
```

List Functions

One of the most important functions among the list functions is `nth($list, $n)`. It's used to fetch a single item from the list. Unlike with JavaScript, Sass lists start counting from 1.

Thus, `nth(10px 20px 30px, 1)` will return 10px as a result.

Another important function is `join`. `join($list1, $list2, [$separator])` is used to generate a new list by combining two lists. Each value in the list counts as a single item, and the function can also be used to make lists out of individual items. The optional `$separator` argument determines which type of list it should be; it can be a space or a comma. If it's left out, the `$list1` type is used.

Another simple yet important function is `length($list)`. It returns the number of items in `$list`. So `length(10 22 33)` is 3.

User-Defined Functions

The `@function` directive is used for defining your own function. This can be useful when you want to perform actions that are not natively supported. `@function` is similar to `@mixin`, except that `@function` returns a result.

The `@return` directive is an important component of `@function`, which has a behavior similar to `return` in JavaScript. It accepts Sass expressions, processes them, and returns the result. Additionally, it stops the function execution after `@return` is triggered.

Consider a simple example of building a function. This example writes a function that generates width per column based on the number of columns provided, as shown in Listing 3-54.

Listing 3-54. Example of a User-Defined Function

```
@function generateGrid($columns) {
  @return percentage(1/$columns);
}
.two-column{
  width:generateGrid(2);
}
```

Output of this code is shown in Listing 3-55.

Listing 3-55. Output of Listing 3-54

```
.two-column {
  width: 50%;
}
```

Output Style

By default, Sass outputs CSS in a nice structured format. But at the same time, it also provides options of various styles. Sass allows you to choose from four output styles that you can specify in the `--style` command-line parameter.

nested

This is the default style of Sass. It shows the CSS styles in normal format. Indentation is per the nesting in the original Sass document, as shown in Listing 3-56.

Listing 3-56. Example of Nested Styles

```
#container {
  color: #000; }
  #container p {
    padding: 10px; }
```

expanded

When this style is selected, the output derived is exactly as it would be if the CSS were handwritten. There won't be any indentation for rules as would be with nested style of output, as shown in Listing 3-57.

Listing 3-57. Example of Expanded Styles

```
#container {
  color: #000;
}

#container p {
  padding: 10px;
}
```

compact

Compact output consumes less space than the previous two styles. It puts all the properties on one single line, with one rule per line, as shown in Listing 3-58.

Listing 3-58. Example of Compact Styles

```
#container {color: #000;}
#container p {padding: 10px;}
```

compressed

The compressed style takes minimum amount of space altogether. It eliminates all white space, as shown in Listing 3-59.

Listing 3-59. Example of Compressed Styles

```
#container {color: #000;}#container p {padding: 10px;}
```

Building Your Own Grid System

In this section, you will build our own grid system that can be used to build responsive web sites. This will help you understand how grid systems work and additionally help you create custom grid systems whenever you need them. A grid system allows content to be arranged vertically and horizontally in a consistent and flexible pattern.

Grid systems are made of two components: rows and columns. Rows are containers that store the columns. Columns determine final structure and arrangement of content.

To start building your own grid, lets first set some required classes and variables. This is shown in Listing 3-60.

Listing 3-60. Setting Initial Classes and Variables

```
// Building custom grid system
$column-spacing:2%;
.col{
  float:left;
  margin-right:$column-spacing;
}
```

This code sets space between the two columns as 2% and defines a col class, which will be used in addition to the column-specific classes. Next, you will create column classes for a variable number of columns. The example supports a maximum of 12 columns, as shown in Listing 3-61.

Listing 3-61. Calculating Various Column Classes

```
// Building custom grid system
$column-spacing:2%;
.col{
  float:left;
  margin-right:$column-spacing;
}

.col-1   { width:percentage(1 / 12) - $column-spacing; }
.col-2   { width:percentage(1 / 6) - $column-spacing; }
.col-3   { width:percentage(1 / 4) - $column-spacing; }
.col-4   { width:percentage(1 / 3) - $column-spacing; }
.col-5   { width:percentage(1 / 2.4) - $column-spacing; }
.col-6   { width:percentage(1 / 2) - $column-spacing; }
.col-7   { width:percentage(1 / 1.714285714285714) - $column-spacing; }
.col-8   { width:percentage(1 / 1.5) - $column-spacing; }
```

```
.col-9   { width:percentage(1 / 1.333333333333333) - $column-spacing; }
.col-10  { width:percentage(1 / 1.2) - $column-spacing; }
.col-11  { width:percentage(1 / 1.090909090909091) - $column-spacing; }
.col-12  { width:percentage(1); }
```

This code generates the output in percentages. You can initially assume that there is only one single column, which is equivalent to 12 cols. So when you want to calculate one single column (col-1), the calculation for this would be

`percentage(1/(total number of cols[12]/desired number of columns[1]) - column spacing;`

You need to subtract the column spacing, as `margin-right` in specified in the `.col` class. In order to calculate the column width for various column configurations, you need to change the value of desired number of columns. The output of this code is shown in Listing 3-62.

Listing 3-62. Output of Listing 3-61

```
.col {
  float: left;
  margin-right: 2%;
}

.col-1 {
  width: 6.33333%;
}

.col-2 {
  width: 14.66667%;
}

.col 3 {
  width: 23%;
}

.col-4 {
  width: 31.33333%;
}

.col-5 {
  width: 39.66667%;
}

.col-6 {
  width: 48%;
}

.col-7 {
  width: 56.33333%;
}

.col-8 {
  width: 64.66667%;
}
```

```
.col-9 {
  width: 73%;
}

.col-10 {
  width: 81.33333%;
}

.col-11 {
  width: 89.66667%;
}

.col-12 {
  width: 100%;
}
```

Now for the final part of this example, you will add styles for the `.row` class, which will act like a container for all the columns. After adding the styles, the final code should look like Listing 3-63.

Listing 3-63. Adding Styles for row

```
// Building custom grid system
$column-spacing:2%;
.row{
  margin-top:$column-spacing;
  &:after{
    clear:both;
  }
}
.col{
  float:left;
  margin-right:$column-spacing;
}

.col-1   { width:percentage(1 / 12) - $column-spacing; }
.col-2   { width:percentage(1 / 6) - $column-spacing; }
.col-3   { width:percentage(1 / 4) - $column-spacing; }
.col-4   { width:percentage(1 / 3) - $column-spacing; }
.col-5   { width:percentage(1 / 2.4) - $column-spacing; }
.col-6   { width:percentage(1 / 2) - $column-spacing; }
.col-7   { width:percentage(1 / 1.714285714285714) - $column-spacing; }
.col-8   { width:percentage(1 / 1.5) - $column-spacing; }
.col-9   { width:percentage(1 / 1.333333333333333) - $column-spacing; }
.col-10  { width:percentage(1 / 1.2) - $column-spacing; }
.col-11  { width:percentage(1 / 1.090909090909091) - $column-spacing; }
.col-12  { width:percentage(1); }
```

The output of this code will look as shown in Listing 3-64.

Listing 3-64. Output of Listing 3-63

```
.row {
  margin-top: 2%;
}

.row:after {
  clear: both;
}

.col {
  float: left;
  margin-right: 2%;
}

.col-1 {
  width: 6.33333%;
}

.col-2 {
  width: 14.66667%;
}

.col-3 {
  width: 23%;
}

.col-4 {
  width: 31.33333%;
}

.col-5 {
  width: 39.66667%;
}

.col-6 {
  width: 48%;
}

.col-7 {
  width: 56.33333%;
}

.col-8 {
  width: 64.66667%;
}

.col-9 {
  width: 73%;
}
```

```
.col-10 {
  width: 81.33333%;
}

.col-11 {
  width: 89.66667%;
}

.col-12 {
  width: 100%;
}
```

Now you can use this generated grid system with the HTML markup by using its classes, as shown in Listing 3-65 and Figure 3-2.

Listing 3-65. Using the Generated Responsive Grid in the HTML (Example)

```
<div class="row">
  <div class="col col-8">
    Far far away, behind the word mountains, far from the countries Vokalia and Consonantia,
    there live the blind texts. Separated they live in Bookmarksgrove right at the coast of
    the Semantics, a large language ocean. A small river named Duden flows by their place
    and supplies it with the necessary regelialia.
  </div>
  <div class="col col-4">
    This is a sidebar area
  </div>
</div>
```

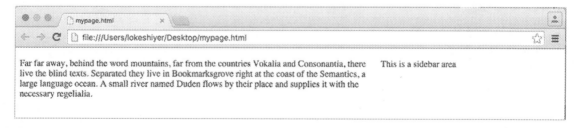

Figure 3-2. *Output of Listing 3-65*

Summary

This chapter explained the advanced topics of Sass, such as including other Sass files using import and using directives, using @media, extending using @extend, using mixins, and some of the commonly used functions provided by Sass and defining a functions using @function.

In addition to these topics, you also learned how to build your own grid system.

In next chapter, you will look into another framework like Sass, which provides similar features and is equally well known.

CHAPTER 4

∎ ∎ ∎

Development with Less

In the previous chapter, you looked into various things you can do with Sass, including various techniques like mixins. In this chapter, you will look into another preprocessor framework that's equally famous, named *Less*.

This chapter explores the following aspects of Less:

- Client and server-side variation of less

- Language features

- Nested rules

- Import directives

- Mixin guards

- Referencing the parent selector

- Using & with guards

- Detached rules

- Merging properties

- Looping mixins

- Functions

Introduction to Less

Less is a preprocessor language that gets compiled into CSS. It was created by Alexis Sellier. Less is along the lines of "SCSS" syntax of Sass, which in turn is like CSS syntax. Less is open source. Less was first written in Ruby; however, in the later versions, it was rewritten in JavaScript. Note that valid CSS is valid Less code. Less provides the following features similar to Sass that you saw in previous chapter like variables, nesting, operators, mixins, and functions; however what makes Less different from other CSS precompilers is its ability to compile in real-time via `less.js` in the browser.

There are two variants of Less, unlike Sass. Less has a client-side variant, which compiles Less code in browsers and a server-side variant that compiles the file server side and then provides it to the browser. Developer can use the client-side variant for developing and testing code. The server-side variant can be used to compile the code, minify it, and then make it production-ready.

A point to keep in mind is that the client-side variant does not generate output. It compiles the code on each browser reload.

Client-Side Variation of Less

To use the client-side variant of Less, you need to download the client-side compiler named less.js, which is available at http://lesscss.org/#download-options. Once it's downloaded, copy it into your working directory. Now let's try some Less code with this Less compiler.

Listing 4-1. An HTML Markup for the Example

```html
<html>
        <head>
                <title>Listing 4-1</title>
                <link type="text/css" rel="stylesheet/less" href="styles1.1.less" />
                <script src="//cdnjs.cloudflare.com/ajax/libs/less.js/2.2.0/less.min.js">
                </script>
        </head>
        <body>
                <p class="impElement">This is my first Less code</p>
        </body>
</html>
```

Listing 4-2. Less Code in styles1.1.less

```css
.impElement{
        background:#666;
        padding:10px;
        border-radius:10px;
}
```

When you run this page, the output will look as shown in Figure 4-1.

Figure 4-1. *Output of Listings 4-1 and 4-2*

■ **Note**   In the example provided in Listing 4-1, we have linked less.js through a content delivery network (CDN). To run this code, you need a web server, otherwise less.js will not load. In case you want to run this example without running a web server, download and link less.js locally.

Server-Side Variant

The client-side variant is good for development and debugging. However, when you're deploying to production, it is advisable to use the server-side variant—i.e., compile the Less code into a browser friendly CSS. To do so, you need to install the lessc compiler. This can be installed using node package manager.

If you don't have node installed, you need to install it first. The procedure for installing Node.js has been well explained here: http://howtonode.org/how-to-install-nodejs.

Once you're done installing Node.js, you are ready to start installing the lessc compiler. Run the command in Listing 4-3 in the terminal.

Listing 4-3. Command for Installing the lessc Compiler

```
npm install -g less
```

You can test if lessc is installed by running the command shown in Listing 4-4.

Listing 4-4. Command to Check if the lessc Command Is Available

```
lessc -v
```

This command will output the version of lessc installed. Now that the lessc compiler has been installed, let's take a look at the procedure for compiling the Less files.

Compiling a Less File

You can compile a Less file using the command shown in Listing 4-5.

Listing 4-5. Command for Invoking the lessc Compiler

```
lessc style.less
```

This command will provide you with output within the terminal itself. If you wish to save the output in a .css file, you need to modify the command by adding a second parameter separated by a space, as shown in Listing 4-6.

Listing 4-6. Command for Invoking the lessc Compiler and Saving Output in Another File

```
lessc style.less style.css
```

The lessc compiler can be invoked with various options. Listings 4-7 through 4-9 show some supported options.

Listing 4-7. The h Option for Help on the lessc Compiler

```
lessc -h
```

Listing 4-8. The include for Including Paths Where Less Will Find Imports

```
lessc -include-path=framework/;lib/
```

Available paths for import can be specified in a list separated by : or ;.

Listing 4-9. Linting Less Code with the lessc Compiler by Using -l

```
lessc -l style.less
```

In addition to these, there are many other options available to apply while invoking lessc compilers. They can be found in the Less documentation here: http://lesscss.org/usage/index.html#command-line-usage-command-line-usage.

In the next section, you will look at features that this language provides.

Language Features

This section covers all the features provided by Less. Many of the features are similar to what you learned in previous chapters; hence, they should be easy to understand.

Variables

Variables in Less are used to store values that would make them available to be used across the code. With variables, you can control the reusable values from single location. In Less, you create variables using the @ symbol. This is demonstrated in Listing 4-10.

Listing 4-10. Example of Declaring and Using Variables in Less

```
@fontColor:#666;
body{
        color:@fontColor;
}
```

Listing 4-11. The Output of Listing 4-10

```
body {
  color: #666;
}
```

Variables are used for more than just assigning values. They can be used in places like selectors, property names, etc. This can be done using interpolation, as shown in Listing 4-12.

Listing 4-12. Example Demonstrating Interpolation

```
@parent: container;
.@{parent} {
  width:100%;
}
```

Listing 4-13. Output of Listing 4-13

```
.container {
  width: 100%;
}
```

Listings 4-14 through 4-18 show some valid examples of variable declarations.

Listing 4-14. Valid Example of Variable Declarations

```
@color: red;
@list: a b c d;
@csv-list: a, b, c, d;
```

Even though variables are similar to constants, their values are changeable. It works on a simple principle that the last declaration wins.

In Less, variables follow the lazy loading pattern, as shown in Listing 4-15. Lazy load technically means that an object can be initialized when it is needed. This is opposite of eager loading, whereby you need to initialize before you use them.

Listing 4-15. Example Demonstrating Lazy Load in Variables

```
.container {
        font-size: @size;
}
@size: 12px;
```

Listing 4-16. Output of Listing 4-15

```
.container {
  font-size: 12px;
}
```

With release of Less version 1.7, it is possible store groups of properties in a variable. The code should be placed between brackets just like with a mixin. This can be called ruleset, as shown in Listing 4-17.

Listing 4-17. Example Demonstrating Storing and Using Rulesets

```
@disclaimer-ruleset: { color: #CCC; font-size: 10px; };
.disclaimer {
        @disclaimer-ruleset();
}
```

In Listing 4-17, we stored a ruleset in a variable and used it inside the disclaimer class. Listing 4-18 shows the render final output.

Listing 4-18. Output of Listing 4-17

```
.disclaimer {
  color: #CCC;
  font-size: 10px;
}
```

Comments

Comments help document your code and make it easier to read and understand. You don't need to cut down on the number of comments to keep the file size smaller. When the file is compiled and the final CSS code is generated, comments are removed.

Adding comments in Less is done same way as in CSS. Comments are written between /* */. You can also write single-line comments by prefixing them with //.

There is a way by which you can notify the compiler that a specific comment is important and it should be allowed in the final compiled version, as shown in Listing 4-19.

Listing 4-19. Telling a Compiler That a Comment Is Important

```
/*!
This needs to come in final output
!*/
```

Mixins

Mixins are reusable blocks of code that can be used across entire code. Mixins can contain full CSS rules. Mixins can be parameterized; i.e., they can accept arguments, which makes them flexible. Mixins are defined in Less as shown in Listing 4-20.

Listing 4-20. Example of Mixins in Less

```
.notification(@value:5px) {
  border-radius: @value;
  padding: @value;
}
.errorLooks{
  .notification;
}
.successLooks{
  .notification(10px);
}
```

In Less, mixins are declared like any class definition. When including a mixin in another rule, you just write the mixin name preceded by a period with the optional parameters within parentheses. Mixins allow you to embed all the properties of one class into another class by simply including the mixin name as one of its properties.

Listing 4-21. Output of Listing 4-20

```
.errorLooks {
  border-radius: 5px;
  padding: 5px;
}
.successLooks {
  border-radius: 10px;
  padding: 10px;
}
```

As you see, the notification extend class has not been rendered in the final output.

In addition to this, you can mix in a class or an ID selector, which is demonstrated in Listing 4-22.

Listing 4-22. Mixing in an ID and Class Together

```
.notification,#notification {
  border-radius: 5px;
  padding: 5px;
}
.errorLooks{
  .notification;
}
.successLooks{
  #notification;
}
```

Listing 4-23. Output of Listing 4-22

```
.notification,
#notification {
  border-radius: 5px;
  padding: 5px;
}
.errorLooks {
  border-radius: 5px;
  padding: 5px;
}
.successLooks {
  border-radius: 5px;
  padding: 5px;
}
```

If you want to create a mixin, but not output it in the rendered .css file, simply append parentheses to it. You can also include selectors in addition to style rules in your mixin definition. This is demonstrated in Listing 4-24.

Listing 4-24. Example Demonstrating How to Include Selectors Inside a Mixin Definition

```
.notification() {
  border-radius: 5px;
  padding: 5px;
  &:hover{
    border:2px solid #fff;
  }
}
.errorLooks{
  .notification;
}
.successLooks{
  .notification;
}
```

Listing 4-25. Output of Listing 4-24

```
.errorLooks {
  border-radius: 5px;
  padding: 5px;
}
.errorLooks:hover {
  border: 2px solid #fff;
}
.successLooks {
  border-radius: 5px;
  padding: 5px;
}
.successLooks:hover {
  border: 2px solid #fff;
}
```

It is not necessary to always include the entire mixin. You can also include specific parts of it as well, for example, the selector inside of it. This is demonstrated in Listing 4-26.

Listing 4-26. Using a Selector Inside a Mixin Inside Another Selector

```
.notification() {
  border-radius: 5px;
  padding: 5px;
  .inner{
      border:2px solid #fff;
  }
}
.errorLooks{
  .notification;
}
.successLooks{
  .notification .inner;
}
```

Listing 4-27. Output of Listing 4-26

```
.errorLooks {
  border-radius: 5px;
  padding: 5px;
}
.errorLooks .inner {
  border: 2px solid #fff;
}
.successLooks {
  border: 2px solid #fff;
}
```

If you observe in Listing 4-27, `.sucessLooks` has only taken the style of the inner styles within the mixin. When you append `!important` after mixin, all properties are included with `important`, as demonstrated in Listing 4-28.

Listing 4-28. Implementation of !important with Mixin

```
.notification() {
        border-radius: 5px;
        padding: 5px;
    .inner{
        border:2px solid #fff;
    }
}
.errorLooks{
  .notification;
}
.successLooks{
  .notification .inner !important;
}
```

Listing 4-29. Output of Listing 4-28

```
.errorLooks {
  border-radius: 5px;
  padding: 5px;
}
.errorLooks .inner {
  border: 2px solid #fff;
}
.successLooks {
  border: 2px solid #fff !important;
}
```

Mixins are like functions in any functional programming language. Thus, like any functional language, they can accept parameters. This is demonstrated in in Listing 4-30, where we have created a parameterized mixin for a border radius that accepts a parameter for a radius.

Listing 4-30. Example Demonstrating Parameterized Mixins

```
.roundedEdges (@radius){
    -webkit-border-radius:@radius;
    -moz-border-radius:@radius;
    -o-border-radius:@radius;
    border-radius:@radius
}

.info{
    font-weight:bold;
    .roundedEdges(50px)
}
```

Listing 4-31. Output of Listing 4-30

```
.info {
  font-weight: bold;
  -webkit-border-radius: 50px;
  -moz-border-radius: 50px;
  -o-border-radius: 50px;
  border-radius: 10px;
}
```

The parameters in mixins can have a default value, which can be used when no parameters are passed when the mixin is invoked. Thus, you can modify the previous example by adding a default value to the parameter radius. This would look like Listing 4-32.

Listing 4-32. Example Demonstrating Default Values for Parameters of a Mixin

```
.roundedEdges (@radius:5px){
    -webkit-border-radius:@radius;
    -moz-border-radius:@radius;
    -o-border-radius:@radius;
    border-radius:@radius
}
```

```less
.info{
    font-weight:bold;
    .roundedEdges(50px);
}

.note{
    font-style:italic;
    .roundedEdges();
}
```

Listing 4-33. Output of Listing 4-32

```less
.info {
  font-weight: bold;
  -webkit-border-radius: 50px;
  -moz-border-radius: 50px;
  -o-border-radius: 50px;
  border-radius: 50px;
}
.note {
  font-style: italic;
  -webkit-border-radius: 5px;
  -moz-border-radius: 5px;
  -o-border-radius: 5px;
  border-radius: 5px;
}
```

Mixins can accept multiple parameters in the form of values separated by semicolons, similar to other programming languages. In Less, a semicolon is used, as the comma has an ambiguous behavior. Commas are used to separate parameters and list items.

Mixins in Less also support overloading. This is demonstrated in Listing 4-34.

Listing 4-34. Example Showing Mixin Overloading

```less
.specialArea(@color; @width) {
    border: 2px dashed @color;
    width: @width;
    color: @color;
}
.specialArea(@color;) {
    color: @color;
}

.fullEmphasis{
    background-color: #BBB;
    .specialArea(#FFF);
}

.sideEmphasis{
    background-color: #BBB;
    .specialArea(#FFF,200px)
}
```

In Listing 4-34, there are two variants of specialArea. One accepts a single parameter—color—and another that accepts two parameters. The output of this code is shown in Listing 4-35.

Listing 4-35. Output of Listing 4-34

```
.fullEmphasis {
  background-color: #BBB;
  color: #FFF;
}
.sideEmphasis {
  background-color: #BBB;
  border: 2px dashed #ffffff;
  width: 200px;
  color: #FFF;
}
```

Less has two special variables called @arguments and @rest.

@arguments

The @arguments variable contains a list of all the arguments passed and existing inside mixins. In Less, lists are values separated by spaces, so you can use @arguments for properties that are separated by spaces like border styles, margins, etc. This is demonstrated in Listing 4-36.

Listing 4-36. Example Demonstrating the Use of @arguments

```
.borderAroundElement(@width:1px; @style:solid; @color: #000){
        border: @arguments;
}
.subsection{
        .borderAroundElement();
}
.impInlineContent{
    .borderAroundElement(2px;dashed;#f00);
}
```

This example provides values for border parameters and then, using @arguments, assigns the values to the border attribute. The output of this listing is shown in Listing 4-37.

Listing 4-37. Output of Listing 4-36

```
.subsection {
  border: 1px solid #000;
}
.impInlineContent {
  border: 2px dashed #f00;
}
```

@rest

@rest gives you flexibility to call mixins with an indefinite number of arguments. This is demonstrated in Listing 4-38.

Listing 4-38. Example Demonstrating the Use of @rest

```
.borderAroundElement(@width:10px; @rest...){
    width: @width;
    border:@rest;
}
.subsection{
        .borderAroundElement(100px;1px solid #666);
}
```

As you see in the previous example, @rest comes in handy when you are passing a list of properties to be assigned.

Returning a Value

Mixins don't return a value like they do in other programming languages. However, you can mimic this behavior using their scope. If a variable is not defined in the caller's scope, it will be copied to the scope of the caller. This is demonstrated in Listing 4-39.

Listing 4-39. Example Demonstrating Returning a Value

```
.setPaddingMarginMixin(){
        @padding: 15px;
    @margin: 30px;
}
.modifiedPMMixin(){
        @margin: 25px;
        padding: @padding;
        margin: @margin;
        .setPaddingMarginMixin();
}
.container{
    .modifiedPMMixin();
}
```

In this code, the value of @padding is returned and then added to the scope of modifiedPMMixin. The output of this code is shown in Listing 4-40.

Listing 4-40. Output of Listing 4-39

```
.container {
  padding: 15px;
  margin: 25px;
}
```

Nested Rules

CSS doesn't reflect this relationship between elements. With Less, your code reflects the relationship between elements and can be written as shown in Listing 4-41.

Listing 4-41. Example of Reflecting the Relationship Between Elements Using Less

```
#sidebar{
    .heading{
        font-weight:bold;
        color:#BBB;
    }
    ul{
        list-style:none;
        li{
            a{
                color: #006;
            }
        }
    }
}
```

Listing 4-42. Output of Listing 4-41

```
#sidebar .heading {
  font-weight: bold;
  color: #BBB;
}
#sidebar ul {
  list-style: none;
}
#sidebar ul li a {
  color: #006;
}
```

This pattern provided by Less is beneficial in the following manner:

- It reduces the code redundancy. You won't be writing same selectors repeatedly for multiple child elements.

- It makes the code readable and maintainable.

Although nesting is a useful feature, it should be used carefully. Nesting causes tight binding between your DOM and CSS code, and thus limits the possibility of overriding rules due to specificity.

Import Directives

Less provides an import directive to import styles from other locations. You can place @import statements anywhere in the code, unlike with CSS, where they need to be at the start of the file.

The behavior of the @import statement may vary depending on the file extension of the imported file.

- If the imported file ends with .css, it will be treated like a normal CSS import and the statement will be left untouched.

- For any other extension, it will be treated like a Less file and will be imported. If the .less extension is not present, it will be appended and the file content will be imported.

Listing 4-43. Example Demonstrating Various Importing Methods

```
@import "filetoimport";
@import "filetoimport.less";
@import "filetoimport.php";
@import "filetoimport.css";
```

In this example, first three methods will treat the file as a Less file and import its content. However the last method will be considered a normal CSS import, since the file name ends with .css".

There are several options that you can include with your imports:

- reference: This will use a Less file but do not output it

- inline: This will include the content of imported file in the output but will not process it

- less: This will treat the file as a Less file, no matter what the file extension

- css: This will treat the file as a CSS file, regardless of file extension

- once: This will include the file only one time (this is the default behavior)

- multiple: This will include the file multiple times

- optional: This will continue compiling when the file is not found

Mixin Guards

Guards are useful when expressions are to be applied on the basis of conditions. They are also known as *conditional mixins.*

Less implements conditional execution using guarded mixins instead of if/else statements, as shown in Listing 4-44.

Listing 4-44. Example Demonstrating Mixin Guards

```
.switchContrast (@color) when (lightness(@color) >= 60%) {
  background-color: #000;
}
.switchContrast (@color) when (lightness(@color) < 60%) {
  background-color: #FFF;
}
```

```
.switchContrast (@color) {
  color: @color;
}
.container{
    .switchContrast(#666);
}
```

Listing 4-44 demonstrates implementing a mixin guard, where the input color lightness is checked and, based on its value, the contrast combination is decided.

Listing 4-45. Output of Listing 4-46

```
.container {
  background-color: #FFF;
  color: #666666;
}
```

Guard supports the following comparison operators: >, <, >=, <=, and =. Listing 4-46 demonstrates one such scenario.

Listing 4-46. Example Demonstrating Use of Comparison Operator in Mixin Guard

```
@mediaType: mobile;
.setScreen (@width) when (@mediaType = mobile) {}
.setScreen (@width) when (@mediaType = desktop) {}
```

Guard also supports logical operators such as and, or, and not. You can use the and keyword to combine guards, as shown in Listing 4-47.

Listing 4-47. Example Demonstrating the and Operator

```
@mediaType: mobile;
@orientation: landscape;
@width: 960px;
.setScreen (@width) when (@mediaType = mobile) and (@orientation="landscape") {}
```

You can use or operators by separating guards with commas, as shown in Listing 4-48.

Listing 4-48. Example Demonstrating the or Operator

```
.setScreen (@width) when (@mediaType = desktop),(@width >= 960) {}
```

You can also use the not operator to negate, as demonstrated in Listing 4-49.

Listing 4-49. Example Demonstrating the not Operator

```
.setScreen (@width) when not (@width >= 960) {}
```

For matching mixins based on value type, you can use the is function. See Listing 4-50.

Listing 4-50. Example Demonstrating isnumber

```
.setVal (@val1; @val2: 0) when (isnumber(@val2)) { ... }
```

The type-checking functions available in Less are as follows:

- `iscolor`
- `iskeyword`
- `isnumber`
- `isstring`
- `isurl`

The default function, explained later, may be used to do a mixin match depending on other mixins.

Listing 4-51. Example Demonstrating "Conditional Mixins"

```
.setVal (@a) when (@a > 0) { ...  }
.setVal (@a) when (additionalCheck()) { ... }
```

Referencing the Parent Selector

Less uses the & symbol to reference the parent of the current selector. The & symbol reverses the nesting order and can extend or merge classes, as shown in Listing 4-52.

Listing 4-52. Example Demonstrating the Parent Selector

```
.button
{
    background:#F00;
    &:hover{
        background: #500;
    }
}
```

Listing 4-53. Output of Listing 4-52

```
.button {
  background: #F00;
}
.button:hover {
  background: #500;
}
```

The & symbol is mainly used to add pseudo-classes to a class. This is demonstrated with a simple example in the previous listing, by adding a `:hover` pseudo-class.

Yet another common scenario where you can use a parent selector is for building a clear fix. This can be done by using the parent selector with `:after`. This is demonstrated in Listing 4-54.

Listing 4-54. Use of the Parent Selector to Build a Clear Fix

```
.clearfix() {
    &:after {
        clear: both;
    }
}
```

```
.column{
    .clearfix;
}
```

Listing 4-55. Output of Listing 4-54

```
.column:after {
  clear: both;
}
```

Less provides pseudo-classes in addition to the ones provided by CSS, namely the extend pseudo-class, which has syntax similar to CSS pseudo-class. The extend pseudo-class helps extend the selector, as shown in Listing 4-56.

Listing 4-56. Example Demonstrating the extend Pseudo-Class

```
.primary{
    color: #00F;
    &:hover {
        color: #006;
    }
}
.secondary:extend(.primary){

}
```

Listing 4-56 extends the primary class by using the extend pseudo-selector provided by Less. The output of this code is shown in Listing 4-57.

Listing 4-57. Output of Listing 4-58

```
.primary,
.secondary {
  color: #00F;
}
.primary:hover {
  color: #006;
}
```

Using & with Guards

Guards can be used along with the & symbol to make a conditional statement.

This is demonstrated in Listing 4-58, where the parent selector is used with a guard to determine which color to use as per the color level passed in as parameter.

Listing 4-58. Example of a Guard with the Parent Selector

```
.colorGenerator(@level) {
    & when(@level>5) {
        color: #600;
    }
```

```
    & when (@level<=5){
        color:#060;
    }
}
p.lead {
    .colorGenerator(6);
}
p.secondLead {
    .colorGenerator(1);
}
```

Listing 4-59. Output of Listing 4-58

```
p.lead {
  color: #600;
}
p.secondLead {
  color: #060;
}
```

Detached Rules and Mixins

Detached rulesets are sets of rules, containing valid Less or CSS code, and stored in a variable. In Less, these detached rulesets can be passed as arguments to a mixin, as shown in Listing 4-60.

Listing 4-60. Example of a Detached Rule

```
@errorStyleSettings: { color: #A00; border: 1px solid #A00 }
```

Detached rules can be called by adding parentheses at the end. When using parentheses, content within the detached ruleset gets copied inside the CSS ruleset. This is demonstrated in Listing 4-61.

Listing 4-61. Adding a Detached Ruleset Within Another Style Declaration

```
@errorStyleSettings: { color: #A00; border: 1px solid #A00; };
.errorDialog{
    @errorStyleSettings();
}
```

Detached rules within mixins can prevent code redundancy. This is most applicable when you need different style rules within different media queries or classes nested within media queries.

Operations on Numbers and Colors

Less provides support for the arithmetic operations like addition, subtraction, multiplication, and division. There is also a provision for placing operations within parentheses to change the order of execution. These operations can be applied on variables, values, and numbers.

Listing 4-62. Example Demonstrating Arithematic Operations

```
.aside{
    width:percentage(1 - (0.4+0.2))
}
```

Listing 4-63. Output of Listing 4-64

```
.aside {
  width: 40%;
}
```

Less also supports color manipulation. These manipulations can be done to values and colors with different units. This is demonstrated in Listing 4-64, where we take a input color and reduce its value by 10%.

Listing 4-64. Example Demonstrating Color Manipulation in Less

```
@color: yellow;
.lighten(@color){
        color : @color - 10%;
}
.contrastContainer{
    .lighten(@color)
}
```

Listing 4-65. Output of Listing 4-64

```
.contrastContainer {
  color: #f5f500;
}
```

Merging Properties

Property merging comes handy with properties that accept comma-separated or space-separated values. Some examples are: borders, backgrounds, transitions, and font-family properties. Properties can be merged by adding a + flag for comma-separated lists or a +_ flag for space-separated lists, placed after the property names to be merged.

Listing 4-66 shows an example of merging comma-separated values. It merges the value of the font property. There are two mixins—fontSettings and fallbackFonts—and the value of fallbackFonts is merged into fontSettings.

Note that if you miss out +: and write it as : instead, content from fallbackFonts will be added on a new line and will override font settings provided by fontSettings.

Listing 4-66. Example Demonstrating Merging Comma-Separated Values

```
.fallbackFonts(){
    font-family+: Helvetica,sans-serif;
}
.fontSettings(){
    font-family+: Calibri;
    .fallbackFonts;
}
```

```
body {
    .fontSettings;
}
```

Listing 4-67. Output of Listing 4-66

```
body {
  font-family: Calibri, Helvetica, sans-serif;
}
```

Looping Mixins

It is possible to have mixins execute recursively. This can be achieved by combining them with mixin guards or patterns.

This is demonstrated in Listing 4-68, which generates 12 column grid using mixin guards and looping.

Listing 4-68. Example Demonstrating Recurrsive Behavior of Mixins

```
.generateGridLayout(12);
.generateGridLayout(@n, @i: 1) when (@i =< @n) {
  .col-@{i} {
    width: (@i * 100% / @n);
  }
  .generateGridLayout(@n, (@i + 1));
}
```

Listing 4-69. Output of Listing 4-68

```
.col-1 {
  width: 8.33333333%;
}
.col-2 {
  width: 16.66666667%;
}
.col-3 {
  width: 25%;
}
.col-4 {
  width: 33.33333333%;
}
.col-5 {
  width: 41.66666667%;
}
.col-6 {
  width: 50%;
}
.col-7 {
  width: 58.33333333%;
}
.col-8 {
  width: 66.66666667%;
}
```

```
.col-9 {
  width: 75%;
}
.col-10 {
  width: 83.33333333%;
}
.col-11 {
  width: 91.66666667%;
}
.col-12 {
  width: 100%;
}
```

Functions

Less provides many in-built functions. With these in-built functions, you can manipulate the values as needed. These can be used within guard expressions. The complete list of functions is at http://lesscss. org/functions/.

We won't be covering all the functions available, but rather cover the functions from different categories. Functions can be categorized on the basis of their input and output. There are mainly the following types of functions:

- Mathematical functions

- Color functions

- List functions

- String functions

- Type functions

The Less functions support native JavaScript functions, since Less is written in JavaScript. Presently, it is possible to evaluate JavaScript expressions inside the Less code; however, this might be removed in future versions.

List Functions

Functions in this category can be used to iterate a CSV list. This category contains two main functions—extract() and length(). extract() as the name suggests is used to get the values from CSV and length() is used to check their length.

The extract function is demonstrated in Listing 4-70, which generates classes for social icons using the extract() function.

Listing 4-70. Example Demonstrating the Use of List Functions

```
@socials: "twitter","facebook","gplus";
.generateSocialIcons(@i) when (@i > 0) {
    .generateSocialIcons((@i - 1));
    @socialName: e(extract(@socials, @i));
    li.@{socialName}{
```

```
        width:16px;height:16px;
        background-image:url("@{socialName}.png");
    }
}
.generateSocialIcons(length(@socials));
```

This example extracts the values from the list named @socials and uses that value to generate specific social classes. The output is shown in Listing 4-71.

Listing 4-71. Output of Listing 4-70

```
li.twitter {
  width: 16px;
  height: 16px;
  background-image: url("twitter.png");
}
li.facebook {
  width: 16px;
  height: 16px;
  background-image: url("facebook.png");
}
li.gplus {
  width: 16px;
  height: 16px;
  background-image: url("gplus.png");
}
```

Color Functions

The color functions provided by Less deal with various kind of operations like color definition, operations, blending, and channel manipulation.

Colors were declared in RGB format in CSS2. An RGB is made of three channels: red, green, and blue. With the arrival of CSS3, there have been new color definitions, such as HSL and HSV, which are similar to RGB values. Less provides supports for various color definition methods and channel manipulation methods. These color declaration methods are demonstrated in Listing 4-72.

Listing 4-72. Example Demonstrating Various Color Declaration Techniques

```
.colorDefinition {
    color: rgb(255,133,75);
    color: rgba(255,133,75,.4);
    color: hsl(76, 80%, 20%);
    color: red;
}
```

In addition to color declaration functions, Less provides two more methods—darken() and lighten()—that can be used to compute a dark or light variant of the input color and intensity provided. This is demonstrated in Listing 4-73.

Listing 4-73. Example Demonstrating the lighten and darken Functions

```
@primaryColor: #00A;
@secondaryColor: #0A0;
.heading{
    color:lighten(@primaryColor,20%);
}
.impNotice{
    color:darken(@primaryColor,35%);
}
.successfulEvent{
    color:lighten(@secondaryColor,10%);
}
```

Listing 4-74. Output of Listing 4-73

```
.heading {
  color: #1111ff;
}
.impNotice {
  color: #000000;
}
.successfulEvent {
  color: #00dd00;
}
```

Having high contrast in your design is an important factor. High contrast not only impacts the usability of design for visually impaired people, but also benefits people with normal vision. However, calculating the correct contrast value is not easy. Less provides the contrast() function, which computes a color that is easily be seen.

The contrast() function can take up to four parameters, from which only the first parameter is required.

- You define the color whose contrast is required as the first parameter.
- The second and third parameters define the dark and light color.
- The last parameter that can be inputted is threshold. The default value of threshold is 43%.

Colors above the threshold value are treated as light, and contrast() returns the dark color defined in the second parameter.

Some other functions provided include:

- saturate()
- desaturate()
- fadein()
- fadeout()
- fade()
- spin()
- mix()
- grayscale()

You can generate a new color by applying color-blending functions that perform basic operations like subtraction on the two colors provided as input.

Some of the color blending functions are:

- `multiply()`
- `screen()`
- `average()`
- `overlay()`
- `hardlight()`
- `softlight()`
- `difference()`
- `exclusion()`
- `negation()`

Let's look at some of these blending functions.

- `multiply()` performs multiplication between two colors.

- `screen()` results in the brightest color among the input color.

- `overlay()` is the `screen()` and `multiply()` functions combined, where the lightness or darkness of the resultant colors depends on the value of first input color.

- `softlight()` is similar to `overlay()`, but it avoids the pure blacks or pure whites in its results.

- `hardlight()` is exactly the opposite of `overlay()`, whereby resultant colors lightness or darkness is determined by the value of second input color.

- `difference()` subtracts the second color from first color on a per channel basis. If a negative value is encountered for any specific channel, it will be inverted.

- `average()` computes the average of two numbers on a per channel basis.

All these functions have been demonstrated in Listing 4-75.

Listing 4-75. Example Demonstrating the Various Color Blending Functions

```
@primaryColor: #00A;
@secondaryColor: #0A0;
@tertiaryColor: #AAA;
.heading{
    color:multiply(@primaryColor,@tertiaryColor);
    color:screen(@primaryColor,@secondaryColor);
    color:overlay(@primaryColor,@tertiaryColor);
    color:softlight(@secondaryColor,@tertiaryColor);
    color:hardlight(@primaryColor,@tertiaryColor);
    color:difference(@primaryColor,@secondaryColor);
    color:average(@primaryColor,@secondaryColor);
}
```

Listing 4-76. Output of Listing 4-75

```
.heading {
  color: #000071;
  color: #0000c6;
  color: #00b700;
  color: #5555c6;
  color: #00aaaa;
  color: #005555;
}
```

Type Functions

Less provides type functions to verify the type of the input value. These functions return `true` if the type of input matches the function's test.

Here are the following type functions:

- `isnumber()`
- `isstring()`,
- `iscolor()`
- `iskeyword()`
- `isurl()`
- `ispixel()`
- `isem()`
- `ispercentage()`
- `isunit()`

`isnumber()` returns `true` if the inputted value is a number; otherwise, it returns `false`.

Listing 4-77. Example Values That Return True or False for isnumber

```
isnumber(#fff);       // false
isnumber("NormalText"); // false
isnumber(1234);       // true
isnumber(56px);       // true
```

`isstring()` returns `true` if the inputted value is a string; otherwise, it returns `false`.

Listing 4-78. Example Values That Return True or False for isstring

```
isstring(red);       // false
isstring("NormalText"); // true
```

`iscolor()` returns `true` if the inputted value is a color; otherwise it returns `false`.

Listing 4-79. Example Values That Return True or False for iscolor

```
iscolor(#fff);      // true
iscolor("NormalText"); // false
```

isurl() returns true if the inputted value is an URL; otherwise, it returns false.

Listing 4-80. Example Values That Return True or False for isurl

```
isurl("NormalText"); // false
isurl(url(...)); // true
```

ispixel() returns truc if thc inputted value is a number in pixel units; otherwise, it returns false.

Listing 4-81. Example Values That Return True or False for ispixel

```
ispixel(1234);      // false
ispixel(56px);      // true
```

isem() returns true if the inputted value is a number in em units; otherwise, it returns false.

Listing 4-82. Example Values That Return True or False for isem

```
isem(56px);      // false
isem(7.8em);     // true
```

ispercentage() returns true if the inputted value is a percentage value; otherwise, it returns false.

Listing 4-83. Example Values That Return True or False for ispercentage

```
ispercentage(56px);      // false
ispercentage(7.8%);      // true
```

isunit() returns true if the inputted value is of same unit as specified in the second parameter; otherwise, it returns false.

Listing 4-84. Example Values That Return True or False for isunit

```
isunit(11px, px);   // true
isunit(2.2%, px);   // false
```

Mathematical Functions

Less provides several mathematical functions to perform various mathematical operations on the values. In this section, we will look at some of these functions.

- ceil() is similar to the version in JavaScript and will round the input number to its highest integer value. For example, ceil(2.4) returns 3.

- floor() rounds the input number to its lowest integer value. For example, floor(2.4) returns 2.

- percentage() converts the input number to a percentage value. For example, percentage(0.5) returns 50%.

- round() rounds the number. It accepts two parameters. The first parameter is the number to be rounded. The second parameter is the decimal place to round to. For example, round(1.67) returns 2 while round(1.67,1) will result in 1.7.

- sqrt() calculates the square root of the input values. Also note that while performing this calculation, the functions retains the unit of the original input. For example, sqrt(25cm) returns 5cm.

- pow() returns the value of the first raised to the power of the second argument. For example, pow(2,2) returns 4.

- mod() calculates the modules of input values. For example, mod(11,6) returns 5.

- min()returns the lowest number among the input values. For example, min(2,1) will return 1.

- max() returns the highest number among the input values. For example, max(2,1) will return 2.

String Functions

Less provides string functions to manipulate strings. In this section, we will look into these functions.

- escape() will URL-encode the special characters found in the string. This function will not URL-encode the following set of characters: ,, /, ?, @, &, +, ', ~, !, and $. For example, escape(x=10) returns x%3D10.

- e() is also known as CSS escaping. It mainly removes the quotes from the input string and returns the string without quotes, which can be used in CSS expression. We used this function in Listing 4-70 for extracting the name of social icons and removed quotes from it.

- replace() is used to replace a string within the given input. This function accepts four parameters:

  - Input string, which is the target on which search and replace are to be performed

  - String/pattern to be replaced

  - Replacement string, which is the string to replace the search pattern with

  - Any optional regular expression flags

For example, replace("Is this planet?", "planet\?", "earth"); will replace the word planet with earth.

Miscellaneous Functions

In addition to the previously mentioned functions, Less also has functions that cannot be categorized in a specific group, as follows:

- color() converts a string containing a color value to an actual color value. This is similar to the e() function of string category. For example, color("#555") returns #555.

- image-size() returns the dimensions of the input image. For example, image-size("image.png") returns 16px 16px. These can be divided into two separate functions—image-width() and image-height(). As the names indicate, the former one returns the width and the latter one returns the height of the image.

- convert() converts the input value to a specific unit as mentioned in second parameter. This function takes two parameters:

  - The input value to be converted with the appropriate unit.

  - A valid unit type.

    For example, the following convert function call convert(5s, "ms") returns 5000ms. Note that while calling this function, the input unit and desired output unit should be compatible. For example, convert(10, ms) will just return 10, which is not a desired result, as the input unit (none in this case) is not compatible with the output type. Compatible means that the units should represent the same type of property.

- default() is used with the guard. It is used to fire the guard when no matching mixin is found as per the input. This is demonstrated in Listing 4-85.

Listing 4-85. Example Demonstrating the default() Function with Guard

```
.font(1){
    font-size: 11px;
}
.font(5){
    font-size: 26px;
}
.font(@size) when (default()) {
    font-size: ~"@{size}px";
}

.header {
  .font(5);
}

.content {
  .font(12);
}
```

In this example, you have three variants of the font mixin, into which it would throw a preset value if the input value is 1 or 5. For other cases, default() returns true in which the value provided is directly used. The output of this code is shown in Listing 4-86.

Listing 4-86. Output of Listing 4-85

```
.header {
  font-size: 26px;
}
.content {
  font-size: 12px;
}
```

- unit() has a different behavior depending on the number of arguments passed. This function can take two parameters. If only one parameter is provided, it will extract and return the numeric value from the input. For example, unit(10px) returns 10. You pass two parameters when you want to assign some unit to the input value. For example, unit(10,px) returns 10px. Note this cannot be used interchangeably with the convert() function.

- get-unit() is used to extract only the units from a given value. If the input provided has any units, only that unit will be returned.

Using Less with External Frameworks

You can use Less along with other well-known frameworks. This section looks at how you can use Less with the following frameworks to customize or extend them:

- Cardinal CSS
- Ionic framework
- Semantic grid system

Cardinal CSS

Cardinal (http://cardinalcss.com/) is a CSS framework like Bootstrap. It is a pure CSS framework, which is mobile-first and modular by nature. It does not include any JavaScript plugins like Bootstrap or Foundation. Cardinal's CSS has been written using Less.

Although the framework is nicely made, its documentation needs a lot of work. You will find lots of useful comments in the Less code framework.

The HTML markup for consuming this framework would look like Listing 4-87.

Listing 4-87. Sample Markup for Consuming the Cardinal Framework

```
<div class="grid">
  <div class="grid-item 1/4">Block 1</div>
  <div class="grid-item 1/4">Block 2</div>
  <div class="grid-item 1/4">Block 3</div>
  <div class="grid-item 1/4">Block 4</div>
</div>
```

Cardinal supports seven types of grids made up of six breakpoints, which are as follows:

- xs: 480px;
- sm: 600px;
- md: 768px;

- lg: 960px;

- xl: 1140px;

- xxl: 1380px;

The Less Cardinal plugin will import Cardinal's Less code before your custom code. This plugin can be installed by executing following command:

```
npm install -g less-plugin-cardinal
```

After installation, the plugin can be used with following command

```
lessc mycode.less --cardinal
```

Ionic and Less

The Ionic (`http://www.ionicframework.com`) framework is used for building hybrid mobile apps, which are like web apps that run like a native app. As these apps are made up of web pages, they can be created using web technologies like HTML, JavaScript, and CSS. Ionic apps are built by using HTML5.

The Less plugin for Ionic is available at `https://github.com/bassjobsen/lessplugin-ionic`. This imports the Ionic Framework code before your custom Less code. After plugin installation, you can simply compile your code with following command:

```
lessc apllication.less application.css -ionic
```

This plugin can be installed by running the following command:

```
npm install -g less-plugin-ionic
```

Semantic Grid System

The Semantic Grid System (`https://github.com/tylertate/semantic.gs`) is a modern and clean approach toward achieving responsive layouts, without any unsemantic classes in the markup. You simply set the column and gutter widths, set the number of columns, and then choose between pixels or percentages. It's primarily created with Less, but also supports SCSS and Stylus.

It's demonstrated in Listing 4-88.

Listing 4-88. Example Demonstrating the Semantic Grid System

```
@import 'grid.less';
@columns: 12;
@column-width: 50;
@gutter-width: 10;
@total-width: 100%;
.main {
    .column(9);
}
.sidebar {
    .column(3);
}
```

Summary

This chapter covered another known precompiler framework, called Less. The chapter covered its various language features, including nesting, mixins, and their guards and various categories of functions provided by this framework.

In next chapter, you will look into another known framework called compass.

■ ■ ■

## CHAPTER 5

Introduction to Compass

In the previous chapters, you looked at two famous precompiling languages—Sass and Less—and learned about the various features they provide. Now you will look into a famous CSS framework that is based on Sass, called Compass.

This chapter explores the following aspects of Compass:

- Installation

- Understanding config.rb

- Responsive grids with Sass and Compass

- Compass and CSS3

- Image sprites and Compass

- Compass extensions

Introduction to Compass

Compass, as described on its web site (http://compass-style.org/), is "an open-source CSS authoring framework".

Compass is a framework built using Sass. Installing Compass in addition to Sass gives you reusable patterns and tools that further reduce the time and efforts you'll need to write CSS.

With Compass you can use CSS3 features like box-shadow, columns, and more with a single statement. Compass will generate the cross-browser compatible CSS for them.

Compass Installation

Compass has similar requirements as Sass does in that it needs Ruby to run. The installation process is explained in Chapter 2. To get started, you need to run command in Listing 5-1, the results of which are shown in Figures 5-1 and 5-2.

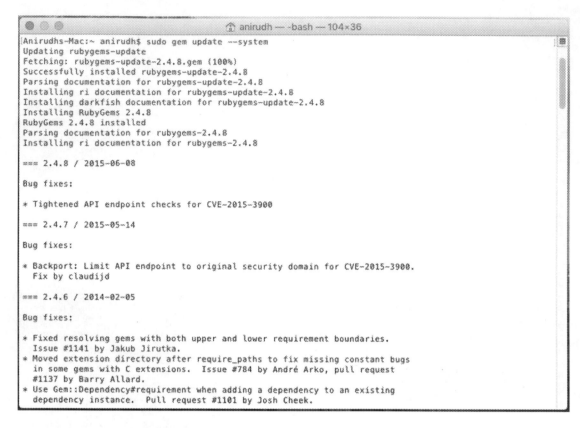

Figure 5-1. *Output of gem update -system*

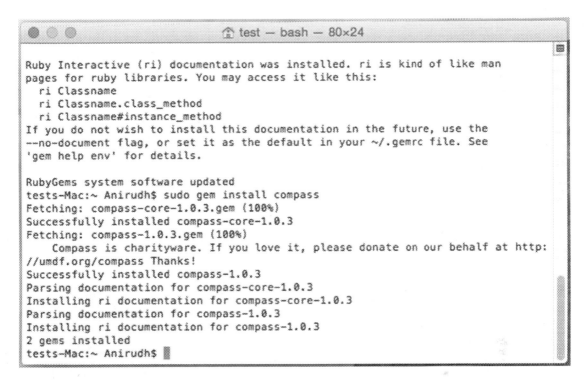

Figure 5-2. Output of sudo gem install *Compass*

Listing 5-1. Command for Installing Compass

```
gem update --system
gem install compass
```

If you want to work on experimental features provided by Compass, you can install the preview version of it by executing the command in Listing 5-2.

Listing 5-2. Command for Installing the Preview Version of Compass

```
gem install compass --pre
```

When you run this command, the output will look as shown in Figure 5-3.

```
Last login: Fri Nov 20 08:26:03 on console
tests-Mac:~ Anirudh$ sudo gem install compass --pre
Password:
Fetching: compass-1.1.0.alpha.3.gem (100%)
    Compass is charityware. If you love it, please donate on our behalf at http://umdf.org/compass Thanks!
Successfully installed compass-1.1.0.alpha.3
Parsing documentation for compass-1.1.0.alpha.3
Installing ri documentation for compass-1.1.0.alpha.3
1 gem installed
tests-Mac:~ Anirudh$
```

Figure 5-3. Output of Listing 5-2

Once you are done installing Compass, you can get started by executing the command shown in Listing 5-3.

Listing 5-3. Command for Creating a Project with Compass

```
compass create <projectName>
```

For Mac users, compass creator Chris Eppstein provides an installer package that can be installed without terminal. This is available at https://github.com/chriseppstein/compass/downloads.

The latest version of Mac OS X seems to have some issues with the previously defined method of installation. You may come across an error such as:

```
ERROR: While executing gem ... (Errno::EPERM)
Operation not permitted - /usr/bin/compass
```

This happens because of the rootless mode introduced in latest OS X. In rootless mode, /usr/bin is not writable even using sudo.

This issue can be solved using the following command:

```
sudo gem install -n /usr/local/bin compass
```

Creating a Project in Compass

To begin, you will create a blank project using Compass. To do so, use the command in Listing 5-4 (the results are shown in Figure 5-4).

Listing 5-4. The Command to Create a Project Using Compass

```
compass create learnCompass
```

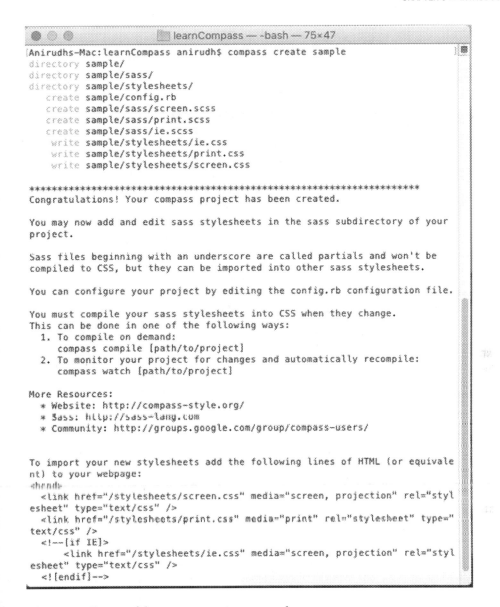

```
[Anirudhs-Mac:learnCompass anirudh$ compass create sample
directory sample/
directory sample/sass/
directory sample/stylesheets/
   create sample/config.rb
   create sample/sass/screen.scss
   create sample/sass/print.scss
   create sample/sass/ie.scss
    write sample/stylesheets/ie.css
    write sample/stylesheets/print.css
    write sample/stylesheets/screen.css


*********************************************************************
Congratulations! Your compass project has been created.

You may now add and edit sass stylesheets in the sass subdirectory of your
project.

Sass files beginning with an underscore are called partials and won't be
compiled to CSS, but they can be imported into other sass stylesheets.

You can configure your project by editing the config.rb configuration file.

You must compile your sass stylesheets into CSS when they change.
This can be done in one of the following ways:
   1. To compile on demand:
      compass compile [path/to/project]
   2. To monitor your project for changes and automatically recompile:
      compass watch [path/to/project]

More Resources:
  * Website: http://compass-style.org/
  * Sass: http://sass-lang.com
  * Community: http://groups.google.com/group/compass-users/


To import your new stylesheets add the following lines of HTML (or equivale
nt) to your webpage:
<head>
  <link href="/stylesheets/screen.css" media="screen, projection" rel="styl
esheet" type="text/css" />
  <link href="/stylesheets/print.css" media="print" rel="stylesheet" type="
text/css" />
  <!--[if IE]>
      <link href="/stylesheets/ie.css" media="screen, projection" rel="styl
esheet" type="text/css" />
  <![endif]-->
```

Figure 5-4. *Output of the compass create command*

This command will create the necessary directory structure and the CSS files. It also creates a config file that configures Compass and Sass options.

GUI-based tools have an option to create compass projects. For example, CodeKit provides an option called Create New Compass Project.

You can customize this default method of creating project, for example, creating project with different folder names. This can be done by providing additional options in the compass create command, as shown in Listing 5-5.

Listing 5-5. Customizing the Project Creation in Compass

```
compass create customProject --sass-dir "scss" --javascripts-dir "scripts"
```

In this command, you are specifying the folder names as per the requirements. These customizations that you provide are saved in config.rb file that is generated in the project.

The compass create command won't create a folder for JavaScript. You need to manually create it.

compass create has an option called --bare that will not create the files and folders that it would otherwise create by default. The created project will just have config.rb file and Sass folder. Figure 5-5 shows the default structure created by the compass create command.

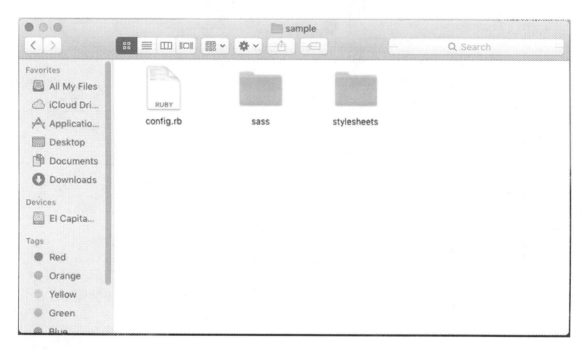

Figure 5-5. *Default structure created by the compass create command*

Understanding config.rb

config.rb is the main file in a Compass project. It defines several important aspects of project such as location of files and how the CSS should be generated from Sass/Scss.

If you open this file in an editor, the content of this file would be something like what's shown in Listing 5-6.

Listing 5-6. Content of the Default config.rb File

```
require 'compass/import-once/activate'
# Require any additional compass plugins here.

# Set this to the root of your project when deployed:
http_path = "/"
css_dir = "stylesheets"
sass_dir = "sass"
images_dir = "images"
javascripts_dir = "javascripts"

# You can select your preferred output style here (can be overridden via the command line):
# output_style = :expanded or :nested or :compact or :compressed

# To enable relative paths to assets via compass helper functions. Uncomment:
# relative_assets = true

# To disable debugging comments that display the original location of your selectors.
Uncomment:
# line_comments = false

# If you prefer the indented syntax, you might want to regenerate this
# project again passing --syntax sass, or you can uncomment this:
# preferred_syntax = :sass
# and then run:
# sass-convert -R --from scss --to sass sass scss && rm -rf sass && mv scss sass
```

When you make changes to the `config.rb` file, it is advisable to clear the `.sass-cache` by either manually deleting the sasscache folder or by running the `compass clean` command.

You can use following command to watch the project changes: `compass watch`

Additional gems for flexible grids, boilerplate frameworks, and so on are available and can be referenced in a project, through `config.rb` file. This is done in the first section of the `config.rb` file. Note however you need to install these addons before you import them into your Compass project.

Let's consider an example where you want to import 960 Grid CSS framework addon. For this, you will have to first install the addon shown in Listing 5-7 (the results are shown in Figure 5-6).

Listing 5-7. Installing Custom Addons in the Compass Project

```
sudo gem install compass-960-plugin
```

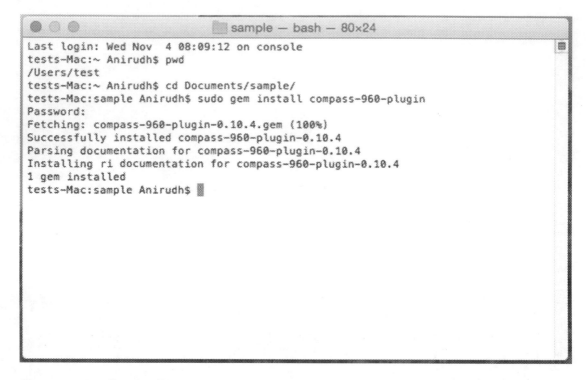

```
● ● ●                    ▦ sample — bash — 80×24
Last login: Wed Nov  4 08:09:12 on console
tests-Mac:~ Anirudh$ pwd
/Users/test
tests-Mac:~ Anirudh$ cd Documents/sample/
tests-Mac:sample Anirudh$ sudo gem install compass-960-plugin
Password:
Fetching: compass-960-plugin-0.10.4.gem (100%)
Successfully installed compass-960-plugin-0.10.4
Parsing documentation for compass-960-plugin-0.10.4
Installing ri documentation for compass-960-plugin-0.10.4
1 gem installed
tests-Mac:sample Anirudh$ ▮
```

Figure 5-6. *Installing an addon in a Compass project*

After installing the addon, the next step is to include it in your project. In case of an existing project, you need to change the first part of `config.rb` where you need to add a `require` statement, as shown in Listing 5-8.

Listing 5-8. Adding require in config.rb

```
require "ninesixty"
```

Once you add this to the config file, you can add `960 grid` to your project by using `@import` statements within your SCSS, as shown in Listing 5-9.

Listing 5-9. Importing the 960 Grid

```
@import "960/grid";
@include grid-system-complete(12);
```

This would add 960 grid system to your SCSS file. Since I created this project using the default `compass create` command, I will be using `screen.scss` as shown in Listing 5-9. Now in order to get all this code in your final CSS, you can simply run the command shown in Listing 5-10 inside the project directory.

Listing 5-10. Command to Compile and Watch the SCSS File in Compass

```
compass watch
```

```
70   /* line 99, ../../../../../Library/Ruby/Gems/2.0.0/gems/compass-960-plugin-0.10.4/stylesheets/960/_grid.sass */
71   .container_12 {
72     margin-left: auto;
73     margin-right: auto;
74     width: 960 ;
75   }
76   /* line 35, ../../../../../Library/Ruby/Gems/2.0.0/gems/compass-960-plugin-0.10.4/stylesheets/960/_grid.sass */
77   .container_12 .grid_1, .container_12 .grid_2, .container_12 .grid_3, .container_12 .grid_4, .container_12 .grid_5, .conta
78     display: inline;
79     float: left;
80     margin-left: 10 ;
81     margin-right: 10 ;
82   }
83   /* line 38, ../../../../../Library/Ruby/Gems/2.0.0/gems/compass-960-plugin-0.10.4/stylesheets/960/_grid.sass */
84   .container_12 .grid_1 {
85     width: 60 ;
86   }
87   /* line 38, ../../../../../Library/Ruby/Gems/2.0.0/gems/compass-960-plugin-0.10.4/stylesheets/960/_grid.sass */
88   .container_12 .grid_2 {
89     width: 140 ;
90   }
91   /* line 38, ../../../../../Library/Ruby/Gems/2.0.0/gems/compass-960-plugin-0.10.4/stylesheets/960/_grid.sass */
92   .container_12 .grid_3 {
93     width: 220 ;
94   }
95   /* line 38, ../../../../../Library/Ruby/Gems/2.0.0/gems/compass-960-plugin-0.10.4/stylesheets/960/_grid.sass */
96   .container_12 .grid_4 {
97     width: 300 ;
98   }
```

Figure 5-7. *The compass watch command will add the 960 grid classes to your stylesheet*

▓ **Note**   If you face conflicts with versions of Sass or Compass after adding these plug-ins, uninstall and reinstall the version of Sass and compass as per the compatibility of plug-in. Additionally, changes in `config.rb` are not being registered by Compass watch while watch is on. It has to be restarted.

In addition to including addons in the project, you can also set folder path for various assets. In config.rb, you have a section similar to what is shown in Listing 5-11.

Listing 5-11. The Section in config.rb That Sets the Path of Various Assets

```
# Set this to the root of your project when deployed:
http_path = "/"
css_dir = "stylesheets"
sass_dir = "sass"
images_dir = "images"
javascripts_dir = "javascripts"
```

You can also set final style of CSS output, which is shown in Listing 5-12.

Listing 5-12. The Section of config.rb Where You Set the CSS Output Style

```
# You can select your preferred output style here (can be overridden via the command line):
# output_style = :expanded or :nested or :compact or :compressed
```

The final section in `config.rb` is enabling relative assets, that is, setting relative path for the assets. This setting is not enabled by default. With this setting turned on, you can specify an image name in CSS and it will know where to find it. You don't have to specify the entire path. So after enabling the relative assets setting by uncommenting the line in `config.rb` it should be as shown in Listing 5-13.

Listing 5-13. The Section of config.rb Where You Set Relative Assets

```
# To enable relative paths to assets via compass helper functions. Uncomment:
relative_assets = true
```

Responsive Grids with Sass and Compass

Responsive grids are very useful tools for development. Chapter 3 discussed grids and how to build them. However, there are some common reasons that developers have against using them.

One of the common reasons is addition of non-semantic classes to the written HTML markup (such as `col-md-8`) when you use bootstrap framework.

Another reason for avoiding the use of grids is that they restrict creativity.

However, with Sass and Compass, you will be working with flexible grid system that can be implemented as desired. Make the design as you desire and then bring it to life using Sass and Compass. You can have flexibility of numbers columns inside your grid.

The advantage of using Sass and Compass grid systems is that they take the burden of complex mathematics off your shoulders. Thus, you can build complex grid systems without knowing much of the math. The example in this chapter uses *Susy* to build the grid system.

Introduction to Susy

Susy is a grid system based on Sass and Compass. It's flexible and simple to use. In addition to its simplicity and flexibility, it generates clean code and is nicely documented.

Susy is available at `http://susy.oddbird.net/`; the site contains good tutorials and reference documentation.

Before you begin the task of building grids, let's clarify one important concept. Susy will help you make the grid and will not automatically generate one.

You define what you are building and then Susy does all calculations. Thus to simply explain, it's like telling Susy, "I want a grid with 12 columns, where each column is 10em wide, having 2em gutter and .5em of padding on both sides of the grid". Then Susy does the calculations to generate this grid.

Getting Susy

In order to get the Susy plug-in for Compass, you need to open terminal and type the command shown in Listing 5-14.

Listing 5-14. The Command for Susy Compass Extension

```
sudo gem install susy
```

This would give the output shown in Figure 5-8.

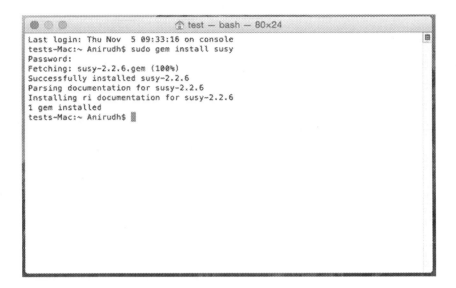

Figure 5-8. *The output of Gem Install Susy*

Using Susy to Your Project

Now that you have Susy for Compass installed, the next step is to include it in the project. In the previous section of this chapter you learned how to include addons through the config.rb file. However, this time you will be creating a new project with an addon included since the beginning. For this, you will use the compass create command with some additional parameters, as shown in Listing 5-15.

Listing 5-15. The command for Creating Compass Project with the Susy Addon

```
compass create sampleSusyProj -r susy -u susy
```

This will output the Compass project as shown in Figure 5-9.

```
● ● ●                      ■ sampleSusyProj — bash — 83×42
tests-Mac:sampleSusyProj Anirudh$ compass create sampleSusyProj -r susy -u susy    ▦
directory sampleSusyProj/
directory sampleSusyProj/sass/
directory sampleSusyProj/stylesheets/
   create sampleSusyProj/config.rb
   create sampleSusyProj/sass/_grids.scss
   create sampleSusyProj/sass/style.scss
    write sampleSusyProj/stylesheets/style.css


********************************************************************
Congratulations! Your compass project has been created.

You may now add and edit sass stylesheets in the sass subdirectory of your project.

Sass files beginning with an underscore are called partials and won't be
compiled to CSS, but they can be imported into other sass stylesheets.

You can configure your project by editing the config.rb configuration file.

You must compile your sass stylesheets into CSS when they change.
This can be done in one of the following ways:
  1. To compile on demand:
     compass compile [path/to/project]
  2. To monitor your project for changes and automatically recompile:
     compass watch [path/to/project]

More Resources:
  * Website: http://compass-style.org/
  * Sass: http://sass-lang.com
  * Community: http://groups.google.com/group/compass-users/


Welcome to Susy! Check out the full documentation online:

    http://susy.oddbird.net/

To import your new stylesheets add the following lines of HTML (or equivalent) to y
our webpage:
<head>
  <link href="/stylesheets/style.css" rel="stylesheet" type="text/css" />
</head>
tests-Mac:sampleSusyProj Anirudh$ ▐
```

Figure 5-9. *Output of the compass create command with additional parammeters for Susy*

After creating the project, you get two files in SCSS directory: _grid.scss and style.scss. Now let's begin setting up the grid.

To set up the grid using Susy, the first thing you need is to define all the Susy-specific variables needed for this task. These are:

- $total-column: The total number of columns

- $column-width: Width of each column

- $gutter-width: Space between each column

- $grid-padding: Space from left and right side for the grid

You will define these properties in _grid.scss. The first line is to import "susy", which is required to pull in all the Susy-related code into _grid.scss.

For this example, you will assume following values for these variables:

- $total-column:12

- $column-width:10em

- $gutter-width:4em

- $grid-padding:4em

The code should look like Listing 5-16.

Listing 5-16. Setting Necessary Parameters for Susy

```
@import "susy";

$susy: (
  columns: 12,
  gutters: 1/5
);
```

Next, you need context for the grid. To do so, you need to set some element as a container element. For this let's assume that the element you want as a container is page. This is done in style.scss, as shown in Listing 5-17.

Listing 5-17. Setting an Element as Container in style.scss

```
@import "grids";

.page{
  @include container;
}
```

This tells Susy that .page will act as a container.

Showing the Grid Background

Susy gives you the ability to see the grid columns of a container in a browser. This can come handy if you want to know how your grid is performing. This can be done by amending a rule, as shown in Listing 5-18.

Listing 5-18. Telling Susy to Show the Grid

```
@import "grids";

.page{
  @include container(show overlay);
  Height:500px; //Height has been set manually to shown grid on an empty page
}
```

The HTML code for this page is shown in Listing 5-19.

Listing 5-19. HTML Markup for Listing 5-18

```
<!DOCTYPE html>
<html>
  <head>
    <title>Sample susy project</title>
    <link rel="stylesheet" type="text/css" href="stylesheets/style.css">
  </head>
  <body>
    <div class="page"></div>
  </body>
</html>
```

The result of this code is shown in Figure 5-10. Note that the grids are visible when you hover over the icon in the top-right corner.

Figure 5-10. *Having a grid overlay*

Next you will set Susy to use the box-sizing model for border-box. You can do this by adding this variable to the grid settings, as shown in Listing 5-20.

Listing 5-20. Adding a Box-Sizing Model to the Grid System Setting

```
@import "susy";

$susy: (
    columns: 12,
    gutters: 1/5,
    global-box-sizing:border-box
);
```

While developing a responsive page or application, the first thing that you should think about is a completely accessible design. That means regardless of the device or its capability, the content should be accessible on your page or application. This certainly does not guarantee the same layout and behavior across all devices.

Now let's take a look at how you can set breakpoints in Susy. A breakpoint in CSS is where the layout changes to suit the size of the viewport. Susy gives you flexibility to define as many breakpoints as you want. Consider two breakpoints. You will define two variables for medium and large inside _grid.scss, as shown in Listing 5-21.

Listing 5-21. Defining Breakpoints in Susy

```
@import "susy";

$susy: (
    columns: 12,
    gutters: 1/5,
    global-box-sizing:border-box
);

// Variables defning breakpoints
$mediumScreen:750px;
$largeScreen:1200px;
```

You might have observed that the example declared only two breakpoints. That is because you will build the sample layout with a mobile first mindset, which would be accessible across various devices regardless of their capabilities and then enhance it for bigger sized viewports.

For this example, you will use a breakpoint plug-in available at `http://breakpoint-sass.com/`. To start using this, you first need to install the plug-in on your system, as shown in Listing 5-22 (the output is in Figure 5-11).

Listing 5-22. Installing the Breakpoint Plug-In

```
gem install breakpoint
```

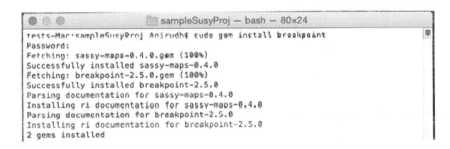

Figure 5-11. *Installing the breakpoint plug-in*

The next step is to include the plug-in in the `config.rb` file of your project using `require "breakpoint`.

After including it in your config file, you need to include it in the SCSS file you are working with `@import "breakpoint"`.

Now you will start using the breakpoint in your code. To do so, let's start by setting `font-size` to 1.5em for the large-screen breakpoint that you defined earlier, as shown in Listing 5-23.

Listing 5-23. Setting the Style for a Large-Screen Breakpoint in _grids.scss

```
@import "susy";
@import "breakpoint";

$susy: (
    columns: 12,
    gutters: 1/5,
```

```
   global-box-sizing:border-box
);

// Variables defning breakpoints value
$mediumScreen:750px;
$largeScreen:1200px;

.page {
   @include breakpoint($largeScreen) {
      font-size: 1.5em;
   }
}
```

This code will generate a media query for the larger screen, as shown in Listing 5-24.

Listing 5-24. Output of Listing 5-23 in style.css

```
@media (min-width: 1200px) {
   /* line 17, ../sass/_grids.scss */
   .page {
      font-size: 1.5em;
   }
}
```

Now let's say you wanted to declare a media query with min and max widths. You can do this by providing the value in a space-separated format. For this, lets modify the value of the $mediumScreen variable. This is shown in Listing 5-25.

Listing 5-25. Setting the Value for a Medium-Screen Breakpoint that has min and max Values in _grids.scss

```
@import "susy";
@import "breakpoint";

$susy: (
columns: 12,
gutters: 1/5,
global-box-sizing:border-box
);

// Variables defning breakpoints value
$mediumScreen:480px 750px;
$largeScreen:1200px;

.page {
   @include breakpoint($largeScreen) {
   font-size: 1.5em;
}
}
@include breakpoint($mediumScreen){
   font-size: 1em;
}
}
```

Listing 5-26. Output of Listing 5-25 in style.css

```
@media (min-width: 480px) and (max-width: 750px) {
/* line 17, ../sass/_grids.scss */
.page {
font-size: 1em;
}
}
```

You can add a media type to the media query definition. The media type value must be the first parameter of the media query. Developers omit the all media type for creating more concise media queries. If you want the all media type to always be available, you need to set `$breakpoint-force-media-all: true;`
You can see such advanced media query in Listing 5-27.

Listing 5-27. Advanced Media Query Specifying Media Type in the Beginning of in_grids.scss

```
@import "susy";
@import "breakpoint";

$susy: (
columns: 12,
gutters: 1/5,
global-box-sizing:border-box
);

// Variables defning breakpoints value
$mediumScreen:480px 750px;
$largeScreen:1200px;
$advancedQuery: 'not screen' 320px;

.page {
   @include breakpoint($largeScreen) {
      font-size: 1.5em;
   }
   @include breakpoint($mediumScreen){
      font-size: 1em;
   }
   @include breakpoint($advancedQuery) {
      color:#777;
   }
}
```

Listing 5-28. Output of Listing 5-27 in style.css

```
@media (min-width: 1200px) {
  /* line 19, ../sass/_grids.scss */
  .page {
    font-size: 1.5em;
  }
}
@media (min-width: 480px) and (max-width: 750px) {
  /* line 19, ../sass/_grids.scss */
```

```
  .page {
    font-size: 1em;
  }
}
@media not screen and (min-width: 320px) {
  /* line 19, ../sass/_grids.scss */
  .page {
    color: #777;
  }
}
```

Multiple features can be combined to form a compound media query. This allows many features to be evaluated, as shown in Listing 5-29.

Listing 5-29. Example Demonstrating a Compound Media Query in _grid.scss

```
@import "susy";
@import "breakpoint";

$susy: (
    columns: 12,
    gutters: 1/5,
    global-box-sizing:border-box
);

// Variables defning breakpoints value
$mediumScreen:480px 750px;
$largeScreen:1200px;
$advancedQuaery: 'not screen' 320px;
$compoundQuery: print (orientation landscape) (min-width 520px);

.page {
    @include breakpoint($largeScreen) {
        font-size: 1.5em;
    }
    @include breakpoint($mediumScreen){
        font-size: 1em;
    }
    @include breakpoint($advancedQuery) {
        color:#777;
    }
    @include breakpoint($compoundQuery) {
        font-weight: bold;
    }
}
```

Listing 5-30. Output of Listing 5-29

```
@media (min-width: 1200px) {
  /* line 19, ../sass/_grids.scss */
  .page {
    font-size: 1.5em;
  }
}
@media (min-width: 480px) and (max-width: 750px) {
  /* line 19, ../sass/_grids.scss */
  .page {
    font-size: 1em;
  }
}
@media not screen and (min-width: 320px) {
  /* line 19, ../sass/_grids.scss */
  .page {
    color: #777;
  }
}
@media print and (orientation: landscape) and (min-width: 520px) {
  /* line 19, ../sass/_grids.scss */
  .page {
    font-weight: bold;
  }
}
```

Compass and CSS3

Compass has become favorite with many developers because it allows them to write a CSS3 features through predefined mixins in single line syntax, which when compiled, generates a stack of properties with proper vendor-prefixing. This is useful as it saves lot of time and the developers don't have to remember all the syntax. In this section, you will look into some of these CSS3 features supported by Compass.

For this, you will first create a new Compass project, as shown in Listing 5-31.

Listing 5-31. Creating a New Compass Project

```
compass create effects
```

After creating the project you will create an HTML file where you can see the output of all the CSS3 features of Compass you are checking. The structure of this file would look like Listing 5-32.

Listing 5-32. Create an HTML File

```
<!DOCTYPE html>
<html>
  <head>
    <title>Built in compass effects</title>
  </head>
  <body>
  </body>
</html>
```

111

Background-Gradient

Compass provides mixins to support different variants of background-gradient, including:

- Linear

- Radial

- Horizontal linear

- Gradient with angle

The HTML for this is shown in Listing 5-33.

Listing 5-33. Modified HTML for background-gradient

```
<!DOCTYPE html>
<html>
  <head>
    <title>Built in compass effects</title>
    <link rel="stylesheet" type="text/css" href="stylesheets/screen.css">
  </head>
  <body>
    <h1>Background Gradient</h1>
    <div class="gradElement"></div>
  </body>
</html>
```

Now you will add code for background-gradient, as shown in Listing 5-34.

Listing 5-34. Code for Background Gradient in screen.scss

```
@import "compass";

.gradElement{
    width:64px;
    height:64px;
    @include background-image(linear-gradient(to bottom right, #FF0000, #888888));
    display:inline-block;
}
```

In the previous code, you first import Compass so that you can get access to the CSS features. You then define the width and height of the element and set its display value to inline-block so that the element is visible. Next you invoke the background-image mixin, which will render the gradient for you. Its syntax is similar to its CSS counterpart, where values are comma- or space-separated. The final CSS of the previous code is shown in Listing 5-35.

Listing 5-35. Output CSS of code in Listing 5-34

```
/* line 9, ../sass/screen.scss */
.gradElement {
width: 64px;
height: 64px;
background-image: url('data:image/svg+xml;base64,PD94bWwgdmVyc2lvbj0iMS4wIiBlbmNvZGluZz0idX
RmLTgiPz4gPHN2ZyB2ZXJzaW9uPSIxLjEiIHhtbG5zPSdodHRwOi8vd3d3LnczLm9yZy8yMDAwL3N2ZyI+PGRlZnM+
```

PGxpbmVhckdyYWRpZW50IGlkPSJncmFkIiBncmFkaWVudFVuaXRzPSJvYmplY3RCb3VuZGluZ0JveCIgeDE9Ij
AuMCIgeTE9IjAuMCIgeDI9IjEuMCIgeTI9IjEuMCI+PHNob3Agb2Zmc2V0PSIwJSIgc3RvcC1jb2xvcjoiI2Zm
MDAwMCIvPjxzdG9wIG9mZnNldD0iMTAwJSIgc3RvcC1jb2xvcjoiIzg4ODg4OCIvPjwvbGluZWFyR3JhZGllbn
Q+PC9kZWZzPjxyZWN0IHg9IjAiIHk9IjAiIHdpZHRoPSIxMDAlIiBoZWlnaHQ9IjEwMCUiIGZpbGw9InVybCgj
Z3JhZCkiIC8+PC9zdmc+IA==');
background-size: 100%;
background-image: -webkit-gradient(linear, 0% 0%, 100% 100%, color-stop(0%, #ff0000), color-stop(100%, #888888));
background-image: -moz-linear-gradient(top, #ff0000, #888888);
background-image: -webkit-linear-gradient(top, #ff0000, #888888);
background-image: linear-gradient(to bottom right, #ff0000, #888888);
display: inline-block;
}

Background Gradient

Figure 5-12. *Output of the linear gradient*

As you see in the final output, Compass adds the necessary vendor prefixing. Similarly, you can also create other types of gradients; for example try to create a radial gradient in Listing 5-36.

Listing 5-36. Creating a Radial Gradient with Compass

```
.radGradElement{
    width:64px;
    height:64px;
    @include background-image(radial-gradient(30px 30px, #FF0000 10px, #888888 30px));
    display:inline-block;
}
```

Background Gradient

Figure 5-13. *Output of the radial gradient*

More examples of background-gradient can be seen here: http://compass-style.org/examples/compass/css3/gradient/.

113

Border Radius

Another commonly used CSS3 feature is border-radius. It's used to give rounded edges to an element. To see this in action, lets add some markup to the HTML file, as shown in Listing 5-37.

Listing 5-37. Additional Markup for the border-radius Markup

```
<h1>Border Radius</h1>
<div class="br1 rounded"></div>
```

Now let's add code to the SCSS file. In the first example, you will see an element that is rounded from all sides in Listing 5-38.

Listing 5-38. Simple Border Radius Mixin Implementation

```
// Code for border radius mixin
.rounded{
    width:64px;
    height:64px;
    display:inline-block;
    background:#FF0000;
}
.br1{
    @include border-radius(30px);
}
```

Listing 5-39. Output of Listing 5-38

```
/* line 23, ../sass/screen.scss */
.rounded {
width: 64px;
height: 64px;
display: inline-block;
background: #FF0000;
}

/* line 29, ../sass/screen.scss */
.br1 {
-moz-border-radius: 30px;
-webkit-border-radius: 30px;
border-radius: 30px;
}
```

In addition to this simple border-radius mixin, Compass provides variants of border-radius mixins by which you can have single or two sides rounded. Let's see an example of each variation. First, you will see the necessary markup to the HTML file, as shown in Listing 5-40.

Listing 5-40. Border Radius Variants

```
<div class="br2 rounded"></div>
<div class="br3 rounded"></div>
```

Next you see the code for the SCSS file shown in Listing 5-41.

Listing 5-41. Border Radius Variants

```
.br2{
  @include border-top-left-radius(30px);
}
.br3{
  @include border-bottom-radius(30px);
}
```

In the previous example, you can see two variations of border radius, one in which only one side is rounded and other where two sides are rounded. The output of the previous code is shown in Listing 5-42.

Listing 5-42. Output of Listing 5-41

```
/* line 32, ../sass/screen.scss */
.br2 {
  -moz-border-radius-topleft: 30px;
  -webkit-border-top-left-radius: 30px;
  border-top-left-radius: 30px;
}

/* line 35, ../sass/screen.scss */
.br3 {
  -moz-border-radius-bottomleft: 30px;
  -webkit-border-bottom-left-radius: 30px;
  border-bottom-left-radius: 30px;
  -moz-border-radius-bottomright: 30px;
  -webkit-border-bottom-right-radius: 30px;
  border-bottom-right-radius: 30px;
}
```

Border Radius

Figure 5-14. *Output of border-radius code from previous listings*

You can see more examples of these on http://compass-style.org/examples/compass/css3/border_radius/.

Opacity

Compass also provides a mixin for opacity by which you can play with transparency of the element. This is demonstrated in Listing 5-43.

Listing 5-43. Opacity Mixin Provided by Compass

```
<h1>Opacity</h1>
<div class="opacity light0"></div>
<div class="opacity light1"></div>
<div class="opacity light2"></div>
<div class="opacity light3"></div>
<div class="opacity light4"></div>
```

Listing 5-44. Opacity Mixin Provided by Compass

```
// Code for opacity mixin
.opacity{
    width:32px;
    height:32px;
    display:inline-block;
    background:#000;
}
.light0{
    @include opacity(0);
}
.light1{
    @include opacity(0.1);
}
.light2{
    @include opacity(0.2);
}
.light3{
    @include opacity(0.3);
}
.light4{
    @include opacity(0.4);
}
```

In this example, you can set the transition of the opacity from transparent to partially opaque by setting different values of opacity. The output of this code is shown in the Listing 5-45.

Listing 5-45. Output of Listing 5-44

```
/* line 40, ../sass/screen.scss */
.opacity {
  width: 32px;
  height: 32px;
  display: inline-block;
  background: #000;
}
```

```
/* line 46, ../sass/screen.scss */
.light0 {
  filter: progid:DXImageTransform.Microsoft.Alpha(Opacity=0);
  opacity: 0;
}

/* line 49, ../sass/screen.scss */
.light1 {
  filter: progid:DXImageTransform.Microsoft.Alpha(Opacity=10);
  opacity: 0.1;
}

/* line 52, ../sass/screen.scss */
.light2 {
  filter: progid:DXImageTransform.Microsoft.Alpha(Opacity=20);
  opacity: 0.2;
}

/* line 55, ../sass/screen.scss */
.light3 {
  filter: progid:DXImageTransform.Microsoft.Alpha(Opacity=30);
  opacity: 0.3;
}

/* line 58, ../sass/screen.scss */
.light4 {
  filter: progid:DXImageTransform.Microsoft.Alpha(Opacity=40);
  opacity: 0.4;
}
```

Figure 5-15. *Output of Listing 5-45*

Text Shadow

The next Compass plug-in you will look at is called text shadow. Compass makes it easy to implement the text shadow plug-in, as shown in Listing 5-46.

Listing 5-46. Text Shadow Implemented Using Compass

```
// Code for text shadow
.singleShadow{
    @include single-text-shadow;
}
```

This code will apply text shadow to the element with the class singleShadow. The output of this code is shown in Listing 5-47.

Listing 5-47. Output of Listing 5-46

```
/* line 63, ../sass/screen.scss */
.singleShadow {
  text-shadow: 0px 0px 1px #aaaaaa;
}
```

It is possible to customize this single text shadow using three variables provided by Compass, which are as follows:

- $default-text-shadow-color: Default color for the shadow

- $default-text-shadow-blur: Default value for blur

- $default-text-shadow-v-offset: Default value for offset of shadow

Listing 5-48. Example Demonstrating the Use of the Comparison Operator in the Mixin Guard

```
$default-text-shadow-color: rgba(255,250,0, 0.6);
$default-text-shadow-blur: 5px;
$default-text-shadow-v-offset: 3px;
.singleShadow{
    @include single-text-shadow;
}
```

Listing 5-49. Output of Listing 5-48

```
.singleShadow {
    text-shadow: 0px 3px 5px rgba(255, 250, 0, 0.6);
}
```

Listing 5-50. HTML for Listing 5-49

```
<h1>Text shadow</h1>
<span class="singleShadow">This is a text with single shadow</span>
```

Text shadow
This is a text with single shadow

Figure 5-16. *Output of Listing*

You can also apply multiple shadows to text, as shown in Listing 5-51.

Listing 5-51. Applying Multiple Shadows to Text

```
.customMultipleshadows {
    @include text-shadow(rgba(0,0,0, 0.2) 1px 1px 0, rgba(10,10,10, 0.2) 2px 2px 0,
rgba(11,11,11, 0.2) 3px 3px 0);
}
```

Listing 5-52. Output of Listing 5-51

```
/* line 69, ../sass/screen.scss */
.customMultipleshadows {
  text-shadow: rgba(0, 0, 0, 0.2) 1px 1px 0, rgba(10, 10, 10, 0.2) 2px 2px 0, rgba(11, 11,
11, 0.2) 3px 3px 0;
}
```

Listing 5-53. HTML for Listing 5-52

```
<h1>Text shadow</h1>
<span class="singleShadow">This is a text with single shadow</span>
<span class="customMultipleshadows">This is a text with custom Multiple shadows</span>
```

Text shadow
This is a text with single shadow This is a text with custom Multiple shadows

Figure 5-17. *Single and multiple text shadows*

Box Shadow

Yet another cool feature of CSS3 supported by Compass is the box shadow. Box shadow is similar to text shadow, but instead of applying it to text, it is applied to a container. This is demonstrated in Listing 5-54.

Listing 5-54. Example Demonstrating Box Shadow Using Compass

```
// Code for box shadow
.shadow{
    width:32px;
    height:32px;
    display:inline-block;
    margin-right:10px;
    background:#CCC;
}
.defaultBoxShadow {
    @include single-box-shadow;
}

.customBoxShadow {
    @include box-shadow(#222 4px 3px 5px);
}

.multipleCustomBoxShadow {
    @include box-shadow(rgba(255,0,0 , 0.5) 0 0 25px, rgba(0,0,0, 0.7) 0 0 6px 2px inset);
}
```

Listing 5-55. Output of Listing 5-54

```
/* line 74, ../sass/screen.scss */
.shadow {
  width: 32px;
  height: 32px;
  display: inline-block;
  margin-right: 10px;
  background: #CCC;
}

/* line 81, ../sass/screen.scss */
.defaultBoxShadow {
  -moz-box-shadow: 0px 5px #333333;
  -webkit-box-shadow: 0px 5px #333333;
  box-shadow: 0px 5px #333333;
}

/* line 85, ../sass/screen.scss */
.customBoxShadow {
  -moz-box-shadow: #222 4px 3px 5px;
  -webkit-box-shadow: #222 4px 3px 5px;
  box-shadow: #222 4px 3px 5px;
}

/* line 89, ../sass/screen.scss */
.multipleCustomBoxShadow {
  -moz-box-shadow: rgba(255, 0, 0, 0.5) 0 0 25px, rgba(0, 0, 0, 0.7) 0 0 6px 2px inset;
  -webkit-box-shadow: rgba(255, 0, 0, 0.5) 0 0 25px, rgba(0, 0, 0, 0.7) 0 0 6px 2px inset;
  box-shadow: rgba(255, 0, 0, 0.5) 0 0 25px, rgba(0, 0, 0, 0.7) 0 0 6px 2px inset;
}
```

Listing 5-56. HTML for Listing 5-54

```
<h1>Box shadow</h1>
<div class='defaultBoxShadow shadow'></div>
<div class='customBoxShadow shadow'></div>
<div class='multipleCustomBoxShadow shadow'></div>
```

This mixin has following parameters that can be configured:

- $default-box-shadow-color: Provides default shadow color

- $default-box-shadow-h-offset: Provides default horizontal offset value

- $default-box-shadow-v-offset: Provides default vertical offset value

- $default-box-shadow-blur: Provides default blur amount

- $default-box-shadow-spread: Provides default spread amount

- $default-box-shadow-inset: Provides default shadow inset amount

Box shadow

Figure 5-18. *Output of Listing 5-46*

Transitions

Compass also provides mixins by which you can implement various CSS3 transitions easily. This is demonstrated in Listing 5-57.

Listing 5-57. Example of a CSS3 Transition Implemented Using the Compass Mixin

```
.transition {
    width: 32px;
    height: 32px;
    display: block;
    margin-bottom: 10px;
}
// Initiate transition by setting property which will have transition
.default{
    background:#F00;
    @include transition-property(all);
}
.default:hover{
    background:#BBB;
}
.withDuration{
    background:#F00;
    @include transition-property(all);
    @include transition-duration(3s);
}
.withDuration:hover{
    background:#BBB;
}
.widthDurationEaseIn{
    background:#F00;
    @include transition-property(all);
    @include transition-duration(3s);
    @include transition-timing-function(ease-out);
}
.widthDurationEaseIn:hover{
    background:#BBB;
}
.widthDelay{
    background:#F00;
    @include transition-property(all);
```

```scss
  @include transition-duration(3s);
  @include transition-timing-function(ease-out);
  @include transition-delay(3s);
}
.widthDelay:hover{
   background:#BBB;
}
```

In this example, you first set the property that will change with transition. In this case, you have applied all changes to any property will take place with transition. In this second example, you set the duration of transition (how much time will the transition take to complete). In the third example, you set the easing attribute for transition (how smoothly the transition will start and end). In the last example, you set the delay (delay after which the transition will begin). The output of this is shown in Listing 5-58.

Listing 5-58. Output of Listing 5-57

```css
/* line 94, ../sass/screen.scss */
.transition {
  width: 32px;
  height: 32px;
  display: block;
  margin-bottom: 10px;
}

/* line 102, ../sass/screen.scss */
.default {
  background: #F00;
  -moz-transition-property: all;
  -o-transition-property: all;
  -webkit-transition-property: all;
  transition-property: all;
}

/* line 106, ../sass/screen.scss */
.default:hover {
  background: #BBB;
}

/* line 109, ../sass/screen.scss */
.withDuration {
  background: #F00;
  -moz-transition-property: all;
  -o-transition-property: all;
  -webkit-transition-property: all;
  transition-property: all;
  -moz-transition-duration: 3s;
  -o-transition-duration: 3s;
  -webkit-transition-duration: 3s;
  transition-duration: 3s;
}
```

```
/* line 114, ../sass/screen.scss */
.withDuration:hover {
  background: #BBB;
}

/* line 117, ../sass/screen.scss */
.widthDurationEaseIn {
  background: #F00;
  -moz-transition-property: all;
  -o-transition-property: all;
  -webkit-transition-property: all;
  transition-property: all;
  -moz-transition-duration: 3s;
  -o-transition-duration: 3s;
  -webkit-transition-duration: 3s;
  transition-duration: 3s;
  -moz-transition-timing-function: ease-out;
  -o-transition-timing-function: ease-out;
  -webkit-transition-timing-function: ease-out;
  transition-timing-function: ease-out;
}

/* line 123, ../sass/screen.scss */
.widthDurationEaseIn:hover {
  background: #BBB;
}

/* line 126, ../sass/screen.scss */
.widthDelay {
  background: #F00;
  -moz-transition-property: all;
  -o-transition-property: all;
  -webkit-transition-property: all;
  transition-property: all;
  -moz-transition-duration: 3s;
  -o-transition-duration: 3s;
  -webkit-transition-duration: 3s;
  transition-duration: 3s;
  -moz-transition-timing-function: ease-out;
  -o-transition-timing-function: ease-out;
  -webkit-transition-timing-function: ease-out;
  transition-timing-function: ease-out;
  -moz-transition-delay: 3s;
  -o-transition-delay: 3s;
  -webkit-transition-delay: 3s;
  transition-delay: 3s;
}

/* line 133, ../sass/screen.scss */
.widthDelay:hover {
  background: #BBB;
}
```

123

Textfield Placeholder

The last example you will see is styling the input field's placeholder text. This is demonstrated in Listing 5-59 with the use of the `input-placeholder` mixin.

Listing 5-59. Example of Styling an Input Field Placeholder

```
// Code for styling input placeholder
input[type="text"] {
    font-size:15px;
    @include input-placeholder {
        color: #AAA;
        font-weight: bold;
        font-size: 15px;
    }
}
```

Listing 5-60. Output of Listing 5-59

```
/* line 138, ../sass/screen.scss */
input[type="text"] {
  font-size: 15px;
}
/* line 61, ../../../../../../Library/Ruby/Gems/2.0.0/gems/compass-core-1.0.3/stylesheets/
compass/css3/_user-interface.scss */
input[type="text"]:-moz-placeholder {
  color: #AAA;
  font-weight: bold;
  font-size: 15px;
}
/* line 64, ../../../../../../Library/Ruby/Gems/2.0.0/gems/compass-core-1.0.3/stylesheets/
compass/css3/_user-interface.scss */
input[type="text"]::-moz-placeholder {
  color: #AAA;
  font-weight: bold;
  font-size: 15px;
}
/* line 67, ../../../../../../Library/Ruby/Gems/2.0.0/gems/compass-core-1.0.3/stylesheets/
compass/css3/_user-interface.scss */
input[type="text"]:-ms-input-placeholder {
  color: #AAA;
  font-weight: bold;
  font-size: 15px;
}
/* line 56, ../../../../../../Library/Ruby/Gems/2.0.0/gems/compass-core-1.0.3/stylesheets/
compass/css3/_user-interface.scss */
input[type="text"]::-webkit-input-placeholder {
  color: #AAA;
  font-weight: bold;
  font-size: 15px;
}
```

This mixin automatically generates the appropriate vendor-prefixed code, which makes implementing such features very easy.

Listing 5-61. HTML code for Listing 5-60

```
<input name='input' placeholder='This is styled input place holder' type='text'>
```

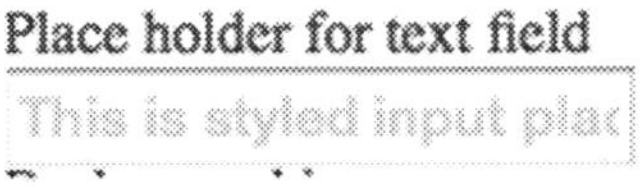

Place holder for text field

This is styled input plac

Figure 5-19. *Output of Listing 5-53*

Image-url()

In CSS, you need to specify relative paths when you specify background images. This is simplified by Compass. Compass provides features by which you can define paths for all the images in config.rb and then while specifying the background image just use the image name. This is demonstrated in the following listings.

Listing 5-62. config.rb for image-url()

```
# Set this to the root of your project when deployed:
http_path = "../"
css_dir = "stylesheets"
sass_dir = "sass"
images_dir = "images"
javascripts_dir = "javascripts"
```

Listing 5-63. Example demonstrating image-url()

```
// Background image using image-url
.bgImage{
    width:128px;
    height:128px;
    background:image-url("facebook.png");
}
```

In this code, image-url will automatically add the relative path to the background image.

Listing 5-64. Output of Listing 5-63

```
/* line 148, ../sass/screen.scss */
.bgImage {
  width: 128px;
  height: 128px;
  background: url('../images/facebook.png?1447046278');
}
```

Image-width()

Instead of manually finding out the width of the background image, you can use the `image-width` function provided by Compass.

This function takes the input of the background image path/name and returns the width in units of px. This is demonstrated in Listing 5-65.

Listing 5-65. Example of Using image-width

```
// Background image using image-url
.bgImage{
  width:image-width("facebook.png");
  height:128px;
  background:image-url("facebook.png");
}
```

The output of this is same as in Listing 5-64.

Image-height()

Similar to the image width function, you have image-height function that returns the height of the image passed to it. This is demonstrated in Listing 5-66.

Listing 5-66. Example of Using image-height

```
// Background image using image-url
.bgImage{
  width:image-width("facebook.png");
  height:image-height("facebook.png");
  background:image-url("facebook.png");
}
```

The output of this is the same as Listing 5-64.

Image Sprites and Compass

Best practices in web development say that it is good to use image sprites instead of using individual images. An image sprite is a single image created by combining all the other images. This single image is then shifted in the visible area with `background-position` property. As this is a single image that gets loaded at the start, there is no delay in seeing the images.

It is a useful technique, requiring a good amount of effort if done manually. Compass makes using image sprites simple by eliminating the effort and complexities involved.

For creating image sprites with compass, you need a folder that will contain all the images to be placed in an image sprite. You will make a folder called `image-sprite` at the root of the project and place the images in it. You will be adding four files to this folder, as shown in Figure 5-20.

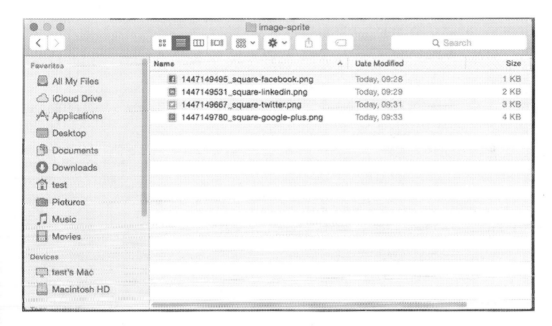

Figure 5-20. *Adddding images to the sprite folder*

Next, you need to import these into the SCSS file. This can be done as shown in Listing 5-67.

Listing 5-67. Generating the Image Sprite

```
// example of creating image sprite
@import "image-loaded/*.png";
.socials{
    @include all-image-loaded-sprites;
}
```

In the previous code, the `import` statement will create the image sprite file. The next `@include` statement will generate the necessary CSS code for using the sprite. The output of this code is shown in Listing 5-68.

Listing 5-68. Output of Listing 5-67

```
/* line 72, image-loaded/*.png */
.image-loaded-sprite, .socials .image-loaded-facebook, .socials .image-loaded-googleplus,
.socials .image-loaded-linkedin, .socials .image-loaded-twitter {
  background-image: url('/images/image-loaded-sbf38a83327.png');
  background-repeat: no-repeat;
}

/* line 84, ../../../../../../Library/Ruby/Gems/2.0.0/gems/compass-core-1.0.3/stylesheets/
compass/utilities/sprites/_base.scss */
.socials .image-loaded-facebook {
  background-position: 0 0;
}
/* line 84, ../../../../../../Library/Ruby/Gems/2.0.0/gems/compass-core-1.0.3/stylesheets/
compass/utilities/sprites/_base.scss */
.socials .image-loaded-googleplus {
  background-position: 0 -128px;
}
/* line 84, ../../../../../../Library/Ruby/Gems/2.0.0/gems/compass-core-1.0.3/stylesheets/
compass/utilities/sprites/_base.scss */
.socials .image-loaded-linkedin {
  background-position: 0 -256px;
}
/* line 84, ../../../../../../Library/Ruby/Gems/2.0.0/gems/compass-core-1.0.3/stylesheets/
compass/utilities/sprites/_base.scss */
.socials .image-loaded-twitter {
  background-position: 0 -384px;
}
```

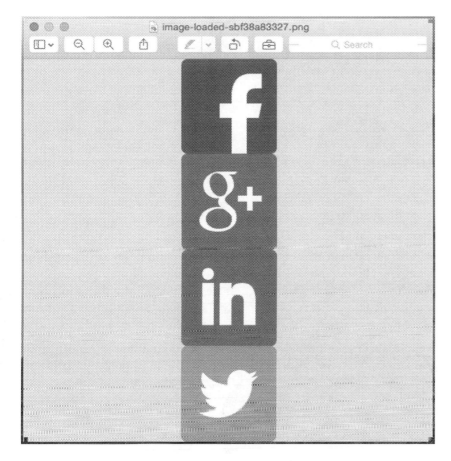

Figure 5-21. Image sprite generated from the previous example

Text Hiding

Compass provides a few mixins to deal with hiding text when using background-image.

The first mixin to look at is the hide-text mixin. It is implemented as shown in Listing 5-69.

Listing 5-69. Example Demonstrating hide-text

```
// example of creating image sprite
@import "image-loaded/*.png";
.socials{
    @include all-image-loaded-sprites;
    @include hide-text;
}
```

In the previous code, the mixin is included to hide text after creating the socials image sprite. The output of this code is shown in Listing 5-70.

Listing 5-70. Output of Listing 5-69

```
.image-loaded-sprite, .socials .image-loaded-facebook, .socials .image-loaded-googleplus,
.socials .image-loaded-linkedin, .socials .image-loaded-twitter {
  background-image: url('/images/image-loaded-sbf38a83327.png');
  background-repeat: no-repeat;
}

/* line 156, ../sass/screen.scss */
.socials {
  text-indent: -119988px;
  overflow: hidden;
  text-align: left;
  text-transform: capitalize;
}
```

This certainly does the job; however, there is catch. When `@include hide-text` is added, it shifts the text. This means the browser is rendering an element with the text in it, 119988px off the screen. This works fine on computers but may cause issues on mobile devices. Hence, Compass provides some alternative techniques.

Compass provides another mixin called `squish-text` to squish the text. This means that the text will be visually hidden but still accessible to screen readers. This is demonstrated in Listing 5-71.

Listing 5-71. Example Demonstrating squish-text

```
// example of creating image sprite
@import "image-loaded/*.png";
.socials{
  @include all-image-loaded-sprites;
  @include squish-text;
  .icons {
    width:128px;
    height:128px;
  }
}
```

Visually this appears the same as the previous example, but unlike the previous example, it is hiding the text inline. This can be seen in Listing 5-72.

Listing 5-72. Output of Listing 5-71

```
/* line 72, image-loaded/*.png */
.image-loaded-sprite, .socials .image-loaded-facebook, .socials .image-loaded-googleplus,
.socials .image-loaded-linkedin, .socials .image-loaded-twitter {
  background-image: url('../images/image-loaded-sbf38a83327.png');
  background-repeat: no-repeat;
}
```

```
/* line 156, ../sass/screen.scss */
.socials {
  font: 0/0 serif;
  text-shadow: none;
  color: transparent;
}
/* line 84, ../../../../../../Library/Ruby/Gems/2.0.0/gems/compass-core-1.0.3/stylesheets/
compass/utilities/sprites/_base.scss */
.socials .image-loaded-facebook {
  background-position: 0 0;
}
/* line 84, ../../../../../../Library/Ruby/Gems/2.0.0/gems/compass-core-1.0.3/stylesheets/
compass/utilities/sprites/_base.scss */
.socials .image-loaded-googleplus {
  background-position: 0 -128px;
}
/* line 84, ../../../../../../Library/Ruby/Gems/2.0.0/gems/compass-core-1.0.3/stylesheets/
compass/utilities/sprites/_base.scss */
.socials .image-loaded-linkedin {
  background-position: 0 -256px;
}
/* line 84, ../../../../../../Library/Ruby/Gems/2.0.0/gems/compass-core-1.0.3/stylesheets/
compass/utilities/sprites/_base.scss */
.socials .image-loaded-twitter {
  background-position: 0 -384px;
}
/* line 159, ../sass/screen.scss */
.socials .icons {
  width: 128px;
  height: 128px;
}
```

Listing 5-73. HTML code for Listing 5-71

```
<h1>Implementation of Image sprite</h1>
<div class="socials">
<div class="image-loaded-facebook icons"></div>
</div>
```

When not working with image sprites, Compass provides a mixin for showing an image instead of text. This is useful in situations when you want to replace a header tag with a logo.

This mixin sets the dimensions of the element according to the size of the image used. This can be seen in Listing 5-74.

Listing 5-74. Example of replace-text-with-dimensions

```
.singleSocial{
    @include replace-text-with-dimensions("../images/facebook.png");
}
```

Listing 5-75. Output of Listing 5-74

```
/* line 161, ../sass/screen.scss */
.singleSocial {
  text-indent: -119988px;
  overflow: hidden;
  text-align: left;
  text-transform: capitalize;
  background-image: url('/images/../images/facebook.png?1447046278');
  background-repeat: no-repeat;
  background-position: 50% 50%;
  width: 128px;
  height: 128px;
}
```

Inline Images with Compass

Inline images embed images directly into the web pages, as per RFC 2397. Data URIs used by inline images are designed to embed data items, as if they were being referred to externally. Using inline images saves HTTP requests.

This is demonstrated in Listing 5-76.

Listing 5-76. Example Demonstrating inline-images

```
.singleSocialInline{
    background-image: inline-image("../images/facebook.png");
}
```

Listing 5-77. Output of Listing 5-76

```
.singleSocialInline {
background-image:        url('data:image/png;base64,iVBORw0KGgoAAAANSUhEUgAAAIAAAACACAYAAADDPm
HLAAAABHNCSVQICAgIfAhkiAAAAAlwSFlzAAALEwAACxMBAJqcGAAABQJJREFUeJzt3dFPm1UcxvHnPaUtOOEoAxEWQ
JawTDenTNOSQYOL3bpoojE6dTdGMyFxF2D4DzbjrSOZiNypGdGMP4CbLbpNoguXkOHF5AK7LGRLhKRkCSWsPa8XQk
LesI6t7+np29/zuSIpOf2RfjmcOrfgwKP34+8Qou5zGhoJDbQppWLez6EAOfqBC5UGcAUhNTY90T+z+WZn44NkciR6Px4+
D2AAUA6oIrmu065zK0OpyeEssB5AMjkSXY5HpxTQZ3U6Kg1XX83n5snU5HBWAcD9ePg8H3xBHPWGCsW+BQBn/
Wf+DLd9geVxHdSvXcU7zwzf3JOfl+BY2E7UHIFueookCb7THIEkd3Kj7Pl0xFOORyC4GIBwDEI4BCMcAhGMAwjEA4
RiAcAxA0AYgHAMQrsr2AJWorWUnXXt6/G10du9nmuoQq4m4mgtiaMqlBx3309p37wacr/MQCftDTV4Z0O9/++jaiaMYg
upsj7NtDKBI7S31+0Lkq+g7vAdOAC+rYQBPKBIOof+jwziZfAEqwBdUMYAnsKetAecGE+horbc9StEYwGM6crANZwff
QqwmYnsUXzCAx9BzqQAPffHUMoSJP8uWkcr4Sw7qfb8W5wURFPfgAA9iWpxti+HoogUg4ZHsU3zGARwiFFM40Jr
BzR7XtUYxgAI/w4fEDONDVbHsMyMYxhAAY3xGD7/4BXbYxjjFAAr49L1u1FaHbY9hgFAN4iIb6Wrzdt8/2GMYxgId4P7G/
Ik/9XgxgC44DnHh9r9+0xSoIBb0OG6l51rR3R3LjD9g9hglwQC2Ojuow/YII/YYIJcMAtnDkRTnvmGcAHvGnavDs7rjtMUqGrwZ6701s
LMn93Lm7jGs30pidu4fbCxksZVawupZDPq9Lcv8bGIBHV8cuo+vPpRcxOpHCn38tGL2f7WIAHu0Gr/5NDWLCxdTJf8uL4Q
BeDQ3mHn6d2lqFiM/TRtZuxg8BHooONvj/J5PmOou4cDHl+7p+/YAAeJl73H50or21/MwbgEY34+/v/O3eXy+bAtxUG4B
GN+HssunYYj7et6fmmMARh2eyeyFje4SCGIBhS5kkV2yMUxAAMMW13L2R6hIAZgWLk+/dvAAIRjAMIxAOEYgHAMQ
HAIRjAMIxAOEYgHAMQDgGIBwDEI4BCMcAhGMAwjEA4RiAcAxAOAQjHAIRjAMIxAOEYgHAMQDgGIJyC1g9sDOG26DXlQqqVtjOGaMwrAFdsz0F2uMq5rBBSY7YHITuUq8fV9fV9ET/
j0u647aHodJyNUav/3/3LmpgIANVsZgquv2h6KSkMDMv4W4ro8PA+tPA10RwNp/LJrkTVD5XYzQSiZ74/cfPVgGgauOG10RwF
sDAa6fGv3d0vh9wjsLRnYCKWJuWfKDXoDHvKueycvX4H7+eubn51v8AYWQlhTwtTVsAAAAASUVORK5CYII=');
}
```

CSS Transform

Compass provides a mixin to support CSS3 transforms. The Compass 2D transform mixins have the same syntax as the CSS 2D Transform functions.

Let's take a look at the configurable parameters for CSS transforms:

- `$default-origin-x`: Sets the default x-origin for transforms
- `$default-origin-y`: Sets the default y-origin for transforms
- `$default-origin-z`: Sets the default z-origin for transforms

All three of these have a default value of 50%.

- `$default-scale-x`: Sets the default multiplier for x-axis scaling
- `$default-scale-y`: Sets the default multiplier for y-axis scaling
- `$default-scale-z`: Sets the default multiplier for z-axis scaling

The default value for these three is 1.25.

- `$default-rotate`: Sets the default angle for rotations
- `$default-vector-x`: Sets the default x-vector for the axis of 3D rotation
- `$default-vector-y`: Sets the default y-vector for the axis of 3D rotation
- `$default-vector-z`: Sets the default z-vector for the axis of 3D rotation
- `$default-translate-x`: Sets the default x-length for translations
- `$default-translate-y`: Sets the default y-length for translations
- `$default-translate-z`: Sets the default z-length for translations
- `$default-skew-x`: Sets the default x-angle for skewing
- `$default-skew-y`: Sets the default y-angle for skewing
- `$default-skew-z`: Sets the default z-angle for skewing

Now we will cover some of the mixins provided by Compass to perform these transformations. The first transformation we will cover is `scale`. This is used to scale elements. This is demonstrated in Listing 5-78.

Listing 5-78. Example Demonstrating the Scale Mixin

```
.elementToScale{
   width:32px;
   height:32px;
   display:block;
   background:#F00;
}
.elementToScale:hover{
   @include scale(2.0);
}
```

In the previous example, you were using the `scale` transform to scale the element two times its original size. The output of this can be seen in Listing 5-79.

Listing 5-79. Output of Listing 5-78

```
/* line 169, ../sass/screen.scss */
.elementToScale {
  width: 32px;
  height: 32px;
  display: block;
  background: #F00;
}

/* line 175, ../sass/screen.scss */
.elementToScale:hover {
  -moz-transform: scale(2, 2);
  -ms-transform: scale(2, 2);
  -webkit-transform: scale(2, 2);
  transform: scale(2, 2);
}
```

Now the next transform you will check is `translate`. Translate is used to move element from one position to other. This is demonstrated in Listing 5-80.

Listing 5-80. Example Demonstrating Translate Transform

```
.elementToTranslate{
    width:32px;
    height:32px;
    display:block;
    background:#F00;
}
.elementToTranslate:hover{
    @include translate(30px);
}
```

In the previous example, you translate the element by 30px on the positive axis of x, y, and z. The output of this is shown in Listing 5-81.

Listing 5-81. Output of Listing 5-80

```
/* line 179, ../sass/screen.scss */
.elementToTranslate {
  width: 32px;
  height: 32px;
  display: block;
  background: #F00;
}

/* line 185, ../sass/screen.scss */
.elementToTranslate:hover {
  -moz-transform: translate(30px, 1em);
  -ms-transform: translate(30px, 1em);
  -webkit-transform: translate(30px, 1em);
  transform: translate(30px, 1em);
}
```

References to more transforms can be found at `http://compass-style.org/reference/compass/css3/transform/`.

Working with Compass Extensions

In this section, you will use the Sass and Compass skills to write a Compass extension, by means of which you can share code with the community. You will explore the design decisions that are required for building an extension, as well as take a look at the associated best practices.

Compass extensions are ways to share Sass scripts so that others can use them. Beyond sharing, they can be used as individual blocks in your framework. Writing a Compass extension is better approach over copy pasting Sass code snippets.

In this example, you'll take make a function that outputs a custom button style and package those in a simple extension called `colorExtension`.

You will first create a directory with the extension name and add a SCSS file with same name inside it. This is the most basic and simplest form of extension, also known as an *ad hoc* extension.

A user can install ad hoc extensions by simply copying the directory into its project's extensions folder. After copying the extension into the proper directory, the extension's Sass files can be imported just like any other Sass file in the project.

For standalone projects, extensions should be placed in an extensions folder at the root of the project folder, such as `projectDirectory/extensions/customButton/`. Please note that Compass does not create this folder automatically. Users have to manually add these.

Next you will add the required code to the extension file. This is shown in Listing 5-82. Please note the name of file and extension mixin are the same for convenience. They may defer in real life scenarios.

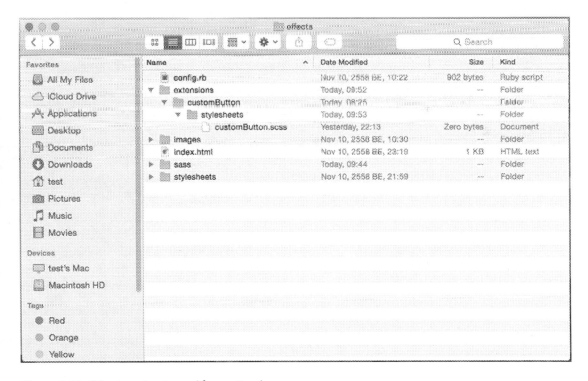

Figure 5-22. Directory structure with an extension

Listing 5-82. Adding Code to the Extension File customButton.scss

```scss
@mixin customButton() {
    cursor: pointer;
    padding: 10px 15px;
    background-color: #eee;
    border: #bbb 1px solid;
    color: #555;
    @include border-radius(25%);
    @include transition-property(all);
    &:hover {
        background-color:#bbb;
    }
}
```

Next, you need to import this in the `screen.scss` file so that you can use it. This is demonstrated in Listing 5-83.

Listing 5-83. Importing the Extension in Your screen.scss

```scss
// Code for custom extension
@import "customButton";
.primaryAction{
    @include customButton;
}
```

In addition to importing the extension into the SCSS file, you have to include the mixin from the extension in the class `.primaryAction`.

The output of this code is shown in Listing 5-84.

Listing 5-84. Output of Listing 5-83

```css
/* line 191, ../sass/screen.scss */
.primaryAction {
  cursor: pointer;
  padding: 10px 15px;
  background-color: #eee;
  border: #bbb 1px solid;
  color: #555;
  -moz-border-radius: 25%;
  -webkit-border-radius: 25%;
  border-radius: 25%;
  -moz-transition-property: all;
  -o-transition-property: all;
  -webkit-transition-property: all;
  transition-property: all;
}
```

```
/* line 9, ../extensions/customButton/stylesheets/customButton.scss */
.primaryAction:hover {
background-color: #bbb;
}
```

You can apply all the concepts of mixins you learned about earlier to the mixin in the extension.

Summary

In this chapter, you learned about the Compass framework, a framework based on Sass. You saw the various features it provides regarding grids, colors, image sprites, and so on. Additionally, you also learned how to create custom extensions in Compass.

Index

■ V, W, X, Y, Z

Get the eBook for only $5!

Why limit yourself?

Now you can take the weightless companion with you wherever you go and access your content on your PC, phone, tablet, or reader.

Since you've purchased this print book, we're happy to offer you the eBook in all 3 formats for just $5.

Convenient and fully searchable, the PDF version enables you to easily find and copy code—or perform examples by quickly toggling between instructions and applications. The MOBI format is ideal for your Kindle, while the ePUB can be utilized on a variety of mobile devices.

To learn more, go to www.apress.com/companion or contact support@apress.com.

Printed in the United States
By Bookmasters